ACCOUNTING CONTROL AND FINANCIAL STRATEGY

Also by Andrew M. McCosh

PRACTICAL CONTROLLERSHIP (*with D. R. Anderson and L. A. Schmidt*)
MANAGEMENT DECISION SUPPORT SYSTEMS (*with Michael S. Scott Morton*)

Accounting Control and Financial Strategy

A Casebook

ANDREW M. McCOSH AND MICHAEL J. EARL

First published 1978 by
THE MACMILLAN PRESS LTD
London and Basingstoke
Associated companies in Delhi
Dublin Hong Kong Johannesburg Lagos
Melbourne New York Singapore and Tokyo

Printed in Hong Kong

British Library Cataloguing in Publication Data

Accounting Control and financial strategy
  1. Corporations – Finance – Case studies
  I. McCosh, Andrew M II. Earl, Michael J
  658.1′5′0722   HG4026

  ISBN 0-333-23355-7
  ISBN 0-333-23356-5   Pbk

Contents

Broad Topic Index

Acknowledgements

The editors and publishers are grateful for the co-operation of G. H. Ray and J. E. Smith in granting permission to reproduce papers 5, 11, 12 and 14, which were articles first published in *Management Accounting*. We are also grateful to *Management Accounting* for their permission to reproduce these articles.

Preface

This selection of cases in financial control and strategy is designed for students of the subject who are not beginners, for use as part of an MBA curriculum, in executive programmes and in third-year accounting courses.

The cases cover such topics as relevant costing, cost control systems, capital investment appraisal procedures, financial analysis and investment centre control systems. Each case has been chosen because it has been proved in years of use to be a practical and useful vehicle for assisting in the development of understanding of the subjects covered. In every case numerical analysis is helpful in approaching a solution to the managerial problem involved. Few of the cases can be intuitively answered without thorough investigation.

All the cases are clearly realistic and thus cannot be labelled as contrived or over-simplified – a common accusation levelled against case studies. They provide for study from integrated perspectives so that issues of organisational behaviour or business policy may be as relevant as financial techniques.

The cases have been extensively classroom-tested, and the book will be accompanied by a full teachers' manual.

1 Associated Biscuit Manufacturers Limited

Associated Biscuit Manufacturers Limited (ABM) was the second largest biscuit company in the United Kingdom. In 1970 the consolidated sales of the company were £53.7 million, of which £32.8 million were produced by the manufacture and sale of biscuits from the company's British factories, £19.1 million from overseas subsidiaries and the remaining £1.8 million were accounted for by a wholly-owned subsidiary engaged in light engineering, producing tins principally for the packaging of biscuits. Exhibit 1 and 2 present financial information about the company, taken from the 1970 annual report.

BACKGROUND OF THE COMPANY AND ITS INDUSTRY

ABM was registered in 1921 to incorporate two biscuit companies, Huntley and Palmers Ltd and Peek Frean & Co. Ltd. A third biscuit company, W & R Jacob & Co. (Liverpool) Ltd was merged with ABM in 1960. During the period between 1960 and 1966 the three companies continued to operate substantially independently of one another, with only a coordinating committee under the Group Board to ensure that commercial and development policies of the companies were not greatly in conflict, and a finance committee to advise the Board on financial policy. In 1966 a small group, representing production, marketing and finance, was set up to form the nucleus of a central management function and to devise a unified strategy for the development of the company.

As a result of this group's recommendations, in 1969 a subsidiary company was formed called Associated Biscuits Limited (ABL), and the UK biscuit manufacturing and sales operations of the three original companies were subsumed into ABL; administratively, ABL became the UK Biscuit Division, with a divisional board and managing director responsible for its operations. Huntley Boorne & Stevens, the engineering company, was established as the Engineering Division, and an Overseas Division was set up to administer ABM's overseas companies; these two divisions, like ABL, were managed by divisional boards each with a managing director. Exhibit 3 presents a summary outline of the organisation structure which came into effect at the beginning of 1969.

Along with the reorganisation there emerged an investment programme for completely modernising the production and distribution systems of ABL. This was to cost over £3 million, and to raise the capital ABM issued debenture stock in the amount of £1.5 million and convertible unsecured loan stock in the amount of £1.635 million. As a preliminary to this modernisation very considerable changes were made in the UK operations of the company's biscuit business: the four factories came directly under the control of one production·director, distribution systems were merged and rationalised, and similarly the selling forces were amalgamated.

ABL held 18 per cent of the British market for biscuits, compared with the 36 per cent share held by United Biscuits. A considerable number of other companies accounted for the remainder of the market. ABM's management had considered the possibility of attempting a major increase in the company's market share but concluded that the *status quo* would be extremely difficult and costly to disturb. The food industry in the UK was in general characterised by a relatively slow but stable growth during the 1960s, and this was especially true of biscuits. ABL's market research department expected market growth in the 1970s to be about 3 per cent per annum by value and 1.5 per cent by tonnage. The following data show the rate of growth in output of the industry during the late 1960s and early 1970s:

	Biscuit sales in thousands of tons	Percentage growth
1966	580.8	–
1967	588.0	1.2
1968	601.2	2.5
1969	591.6	(1.6)
1970	596.8	0.9

The industry had experienced considerable escalation in wage and overhead costs, and a sharply increasing trend in the costs of basic raw materials, especially oils and fats, sugar and cocoa. The industry was a substantial employer of female labour; thus, the progress towards equal wages for women was an important factor in the industry's cost structure. Britain's prospective entry into the EEC was expected to have a very marked effect on the food industry. During the transitional period between 1973 and 1978 patterns of consumption were expected to change considerably, thereby demanding from food manufacturers response to much more rapid change than they had typically experienced in the past. Cereal prices for example were anticipated to be a major item causing changes in patterns of consumption: the EEC's minimum import prices were about 60 per cent higher than the prevailing world prices at that time, so that costs for the sectors of the industry using cereals to a large extent, such as milling and baking, were expected to rise rapidly.

During the 1960s the strategic balance of power in the food industry had been altered by the emergence of the large multiple food retailers. These companies were able to obtain large discounts through centralised bulk purchasing from manufacturers. Moreover, this trend intensified with the widespread adoption of 'own-label' brands for which manufacturers operated on low profit margins, directly in competition with their own higher-priced brands.

At the time of announcing the prospective reorganisation of the Group in 1968, the Chairman of ABM, Mr Alan Palmer, affirmed top management's intention to follow a policy of consolidation and expansion with the following statement:

> That we should plan actively and aggressively for profitable expansion is we hope fully accepted. This policy holds good whether we see ourselves continuing independently or as a willing or unwilling subject of take-over.[1] Such expansion should be part of a well considered, fully discussed and agreed long-range plan covering the Group as a whole. Due to the overriding priority of undertaking the reshaping of the Group into its new form of three autonomous divisions this has not to date been tackled fundamentally and conclusively, and this needs to be done.

Mr Christopher Barber was Financial Director of ABM, and in addition he had a dual role as Financial Director of ABL, the UK Biscuit Division. As part of the overall planning of the company's future he was directly concerned with establishing for the Group a financial strategy, and relating this to profitability objectives of the main operating units and the criteria and policies followed in respect to the appraisal of proposed new investment.

---

[1] The food industry in the latter part of the 1960s had seen a large number of takeovers and mergers, and some companies in particular were pursuing aggressive takeover strategies for growth. ABM was still a family-dominated company in its top management, but the combined holdings of common shares of the members of the various families involved amounted to about 35 per cent of the issued shares. Thus, ABM was not securely in control of its future destiny in terms of the ownership of the company.

FORMULATION OF FINANCIAL STRATEGY AND POLICY

Initially a rough estimate of the Group's future requirements for funds was made, and the likely availability of funds assessed. There emerged from this the preliminary conclusion that requirements during the next few years would have to be tailored to comply with the limitation of funds from readily available sources. A factor in this situation was an unexpected drain on the company's resources caused by a move to new premises of the Engineering Division (Huntley Boorne & Stevens). Production control problems at the new plant had been of such an order as to cause a substantial build-up of working capital and a loss of expected sales. The only course open to Mr Barber at the time was to divert funds from the modernisation programme of the UK Biscuit Division, with a consequent rescheduling of that programme.

Long-term borrowing of ABM was restricted by the Articles of Association of the Company, which limited borrowing in relation to the issued share capital and reserves, and by the conditions of debenture trust deeds which imposed limits in relation to equity and retained earnings and the cover required for interest on debentures. Until 1973, when the loan stock would be open to conversion, little prospect for change in the situation was foreseen. At that time, in the event of conversion, the debt burden would be eased and simultaneously the share capital would be increased, thereby releasing some £3 million of additional long-term debt capacity.[2]

The present overdraft limit of ABM was £4 million. While Mr Barber felt sure that this could be increased, he was intent on keeping this possibility in reserve as a cover against future contingencies.

Therefore, in the immediate future ABM would have to rely primarily on the internal generation of funds or on the issue of new shares of ordinary capital. This latter avenue could be pursued by means of an acquisition strategy, which in turn could potentially increase the internal generation of funds by the addition of the operating flows of the acquired company, and perhaps also increase the combined debt capacity of the overall Group. However, it was noted that in the process of acquisition an offer could generally be expected to be greater than the market valuation of the acquired company; this would result in a post-takeover dilution of ABM's earnings per share unless either ABM's price-earnings ratio were greater than that of the company being acquired, or some immediate synergy could be anticipated in terms of a greater earnings stream from the combined companies than from the two earnings streams of the companies under a separate existence. Clearly, then, if ABM were to have available as a reasonable option for future financing policy the issue of new shares, either on the open market or through the vehicle of acquisition, it was essential to maintain a favourable price-earnings ratio. This focused thinking on the definition of financial and profitability objectives for the Group as a whole, and eventually it was accepted that the appropriate way of expressing and thinking about these was to adopt as a central objective the rate of growth of net earnings per share. One member of the central finance staff of the company expressed the argument as follows:

> After all, a high expected future rate of growth of net earnings per share is the one factor above all others for which the stock market awards a high price-earnings ratio. And having a high price-earnings ratio gives a company much greater flexibility of action when it comes to mergers, acquisitions or the raising of new capital.

Establishing a Group Profit Objective

As a beginning point it was suggested that a 10 per cent per annum growth rate in net earnings per share should be adopted as a Group profitability objective. After further

---

[2] The convertible unsecured loan stock was convertible on 30 June 1973, 1974 and 1975 at the rate of £34, £33 and £32 nominal amount of ordinary share capital per £100 of loan stock.

reflection, however, disagreement began to be expressed about this rate, and a study of the performance of some other major companies in the food industry was undertaken. Exhibit 4 tabulates the performance of a selection from the 27 companies included in this study. It was discovered that nearly half of the companies examined showed a decline rather than a growth in earnings per share during the period from 1959 to 1968, while it was indeed exceptional for any company to sustain a growth rate as high as 10 per cent. On a five-year basis it was true that ABM led the field, with a growth rate of more than 20 per cent, but it was immediately apparent that this figure derived from the exceptionally poor performance of ABM in 1964, the selected base year, rather than from exceptional achievements thereafter.

It was concluded that a 10 per cent growth rate was over-optimistic, while 12.5 per cent was quite unattainable. A target of 8 per cent was considered to be nearer to the realistic potential of the Group. This judgement was substantiated by an external adviser in the City, who expressed the view: '. . . a 10 per cent rate of growth in net earnings per share is aiming too high. Few larger companies will ever be able to sustain a growth of this magnitude. . . . While ABM has some elements which could lead to a satisfactory growth rate, it is missing two of the most important: the ability to step up gearing, and major participation in any rapidly growing industry.'

In December 1969 it was agreed by ABM's top management that the overall profitability objective of the Group should be stated as the achievement of an 8 per cent per annum growth rate in net earnings per share.

Derivation of Divisional Profitability Objectives

The next task undertaken by the planning group under Mr Barber's direction was to translate the Group profitability objective into a set of objectives for the company's divisions and main operating units within divisions. In doing so, it was first agreed as a principle that the profits to be achieved by the divisions should add up to the profit requirement of the Group. Furthermore, it was recognised that some restraint on the investment used to produce the required profit would have to be expressed. This led to the idea of establishing a dual objective for each division, including both a profit objective and an objective rate of return on capital employed.

In terms of the latter objective, and subsequently in the measurement of divisional performance, it was decided that 'capital employed' should be defined as: fixed assets valued at the historical cost of their acquisition plus net working capital exclusive of cash. Capital employed in trade investments was also included in the divisional asset base at the acquisition cost of the shares. With regard to cash, it was argued that cash was in fact capital *not* employed, and was in any case principally controlled at the Group level.

Other bases for the valuation of fixed assets were considered before finally choosing gross book value. For example, it was considered that net book value would give an untrue picture[3] of the trend of performance over time. And the possibility of using the EIU indices for food machinery and buildings to convert assets to a replacement value was examined; however, on this basis one ended up with a higher value for old than for new equipment, yet the new equipment was demonstrably more productive; thus indicating this method of valuation to be clearly unsound from an economic standpoint.

The planning group chose a base year of 1968 as a starting point from which to construct the divisional profit and return on capital objectives. This year was selected for three reasons: it was the most recent year for which results were available when the group began the planning exercise; it marked the last year of operations under the old

---

[3] Especially in view of the heavy investment programme of modernisation. Net book valuation would have made the modernisation look a poor investment *vis-à-vis* the existing plant and equipment.

organisation structure; and it was from a historical standpoint a reasonably high point in terms of performance so that targets derived using that base would not be too easily attainable.

Derivation of profit objectives for the divisions from the overall Group profitability objective is demonstrated in Exhibit 5, and explained in the notes to the exhibit. This document was light-heartedly referred to as 'the long-range plan', so named because of its physical dimensions on paper.

The profit objectives thus derived were compared with the profits implied by the application of the target return on capital employed. The average return on capital employed for the Group for the previous three years, calculated on the basis of the definition used by ABM as already described, had been:[4]

	1970	1969	1968
Average ROCE for the Group (after deduction of overseas minority interests)	4.05%	4.16%	6.68%

Members of ABM's financial staff had discussed the problem of setting targets for return on capital with the financial planners of other major public companies, in particular with the staff of one of the major chemical companies. This latter company, after considerable study and analysis, had set as their target an average return before tax and interest of 12.5 per cent. ABM accepted this target, but adjusted it to an after-interest rate of 10.5 per cent. Because of exceptional circumstances the Britannia Biscuit Company (BBC), ABM's Indian subsidiary, was consistently expected to earn a return on capital substantially in excess of this figure. Accordingly, it was decided that a common return on capital target of 9 per cent should be set for all the other subsidiaries, so that when combined with the expected rate of return of BBC the average return of 10.5 per cent would be achieved for the Group. For financial planning purposes it was decided that the subsidiaries other than BBC should be expected to attain the 9 per cent return by 1975.

Combining the profit objectives of the divisions, or main operating units within divisions, and the 9 per cent return objective – i.e. assuming that they would both be accomplished in 1975 – allowed the calculation of the expected capital to be employed in 1975, and a comparison with the capital actually employed in 1969. These figures were as follows:

	1975 Profit Objective	1975 Capital Employed	1969 Capital Employed	Percentage Increase 1969–75
ABL	2,337	26,000	25,044	3.8
HB & S	206	2,290	2,207	3.8
PF (Canada)	244	2,720	2,380	14.3
PF (Australia)	169	1,880	1,651	13.9

All of the subsidiaries, especially the British ones, were already close to their capital employed ceilings of 1975; in fact, ABL was expected to exceed capital employed of £26 million in 1970. Therefore, divisional managements were going to have to find ways of releasing and conserving capital between 1969 and 1975, while at the same time working towards their profit objectives.

The planning group was now faced with the problem of integrating the two approaches to setting targets for the intervening years between 1969 and 1975. The

---

[4] It is not possible to connect these figures with the before-tax return on capital employed reported in the company's annual report, and reproduced in Exhibit 1. The figures used in planning and performance measurement were based on the gross book value of assets, along with some other adjustments.

approach adopted was explained as follows, and shown for ABL in Exhibit 6:

> If we set what we call 'dual objectives' as we have done, this means that for a given capital employed there are two profits, one which meets the first objective of an amount required to achieve the Group's profit objective and the other of which achieves 9 per cent on the divisional capital employed. In the case of all our Divisions, the first objective appears to be easier to meet than the second. You will see that we have shown three objectives for each year: one is the first objective of profit only, the second is the objective of 9 per cent on capital employed throughout, and the third is the one which starts from the profit objective in 1968 and ends up by achieving 9 per cent on capital employed in 1975. What we have done here is to look at the profit objective in 1975 and say that if that is to be also the 9 per cent objective, the capital employed at that stage must be a certain figure and we have then pitched the dual objective line such that we are always earning 9 per cent on any excess of the actual capital employed over that calculated capital for 1975 in addition to profit objective.

In this way, divisional profit objectives were established which would achieve the Group earnings per share objective and, by 1975 and subsequently, also satisfy the Group return on capital employed objective.

FINANCIAL PLANNING AND REPORTING SYSTEMS

The company had an established system of financial planning which generated a four-year profit plan, along with capital budgets and cash-flow projections. The planning system operated in such a way that the divisions compiled their respective plans, and these were reviewed and ultimately approved at Group headquarters. The divisions, in their planning process, gave effect to policy changes which had already been agreed upon, but of course Group management was continually working on the possibility of further changes of strategy and policy. The financial plans produced by the divisions served as a basis from which to experiment with the effects of possible changes in strategies and policies.

The first year of the four-year plan was the operating budget. In effect, the budget was arrived at by a different process from the plan; it was built up from the 'grass roots', and involved the managers right down to the level of the smallest cost centre.

Budgeted and planned profits of the divisions did not reflect the profit and return on capital objectives arrived at in the Group planning process described earlier. Mr Barber wondered if there was any real purpose in confronting a divisional management with the 'gap' between the profit performance as expressed in their plans and the objectives derived at the Group level; and if so, what kind of analysis of this 'gap' would be appropriate.

Capital Budgeting Policy and Criteria

Mr Barber, now in his role as Financial Director of ABL, was reviewing the policy and criteria in respect to capital budgeting, and wondering how the established policy in this area fitted with the division's profit and return on capital objectives. The policy had been set in 1968, and the tenor of management's thinking at that time had been expressed by the Managing Director of ABL as follows:

> It is the intention of the Division actively and continuously to seek out avenues for cost improvement obtainable through capital expenditure, with particular reference to the policy of developing capital intensive, high labour productivity operations. The Managing Director wishes Works Directors to take responsibility

for bringing forward proposals for worthwhile developments to this end.

Works Directors are reminded that all such proposals must come forward to the Managing Director's Planning Committee accompanied by carefully prepared evaluations, using in most cases, D.C.F. calculations. They (or their Management Accountants) are invited to consult the Group Treasurer on the preparation of evaluation forms.

Cut-off rates for investment were specified as:

(a) for projects reasonably certain and having little risk, e.g. proved machinery etc.   10 per cent

(b) projects mildly speculative, e.g. plant new to the company, capacity and manning of which is known only by specification.   15 per cent

(c) projects speculative, e.g. experimental plant and specialist plant for new lines.   25 per cent

Mr Barber recalled that originally the minimum cut-off rate to justify an investment had been an 8 per cent expected return. Prior to 1967 the company's thinking on suitable rates of return to its investments was conditioned by the rates which other public companies and the nationalised industries appeared to find acceptable. This thinking indicated a rate of about 8 per cent. During the period of reorganisation within the Group, however, the planning group had become interested in the question of appropriate rates of return to the capital which was being invested. It was no longer felt that a simple comparative study was sufficient as a means of arriving at a rate. This change in thinking was, in part, brought about by a change in the financial environment of the Group. It had, formerly, regarded itself as being well placed with respect to finance, but after the modernisation decision, the company was faced with a period of 'tighter' finance in which both internal management of working capital and external availability of funds were important factors. It was decided that academic experts should be consulted on these matters, especially seeking an assessment of the company's cost of capital. In due course a report was received from the experts, the content of which is reproduced as Exhibit 7.

The planning group had accepted this reasoning, and adopted the rate of 10 per cent as the basis for determining the acceptability of projects with little or no risk. It was thought, however, that some allowance should be made for the riskiness of projects; experience suggested a rate of 15 per cent for moderately speculative projects, and one of 25 per cent for projects which were considered definitely speculative.

Capital budgets were prepared annually by the divisions and approved by the Chairman's Committee and the Board. The budgets were 'built up from the floor', that is, people within the divisions said what they required, and these proposals were then discussed at technical meetings at plant level where the chief engineers 'weeded out' the less suitable. At divisional headquarters the Production Director was responsible for consolidating the requests from the factories, and he himself made some selection from these in order to 'keep within sight' of his forecasts.

Inclusion of a project in the annual budget was not intended to be a guarantee that the funds for its execution would be made available. All projects, both those included in the budget and those which arose after the budget had been prepared, were intended to be subjected to a procedure of evaluation and approval designed to determine the acceptability of the expected returns on the funds invested. But in a great number of cases, either this evaluation was not carried out or the rate of return actually accepted was below the specified minima. In most of these cases the projects had been justified on the grounds that they were essential to the completion of some refurbishing of a part of the plant, or that a previous expenditure had necessitated this particular follow-up. This could be explained in part by the fact that many projects gained approval in principle as part of some major programme of investment which was accepted as a whole. At the time of actual expenditure, although the expected returns to the particular project did not reach the specified minima, the investment was approved as an element of the major programme. Mr Barber felt that it was indeed a very perplexing question: how could an essential modification to plant be refused, even if its D.C.F. yield only promised 4 per cent? This in fact was the figure from a recent proposal which had been authorised for expenditure.

EXHIBIT 1   The Associated Biscuit Manufacturers Ltd and Subsidiaries

Five-year Summary of Operations (£'ooo)

	1970	1969	1968	1967	1966
Sales: UK Companies –					
Biscuit manufacture	32,835	31,610	31,067	29,755	31,319
Packaging and light engineering	1,788	1,640	1,478		
Overseas Companies	19,054	16,999	14,950	13,410	12,541
	53,677	50,249	47,495	43,165	43,860
Trading Profit: UK Companies –					
Biscuit manufacture	1,270	1,302	1,478		
Packaging and light engineering	(243)	(356)	(33)		
Overseas Companies	1,606	1,542	1,344		
	2,633	2,488	2,789		
Other Income less Charges	205	100	141		
	2,838	2,588	2,930		
Interest Payable	649	610	454		
	2,189	1,978	2,476	1,990	2,295
Taxation	1,097	1,154	1,284	1,123	1,189
	1,092	824	1,192	867	1,106
Minority Interest (47% of Indian Subsidiary)	248	249	182	129	172
Net Profit of the Company	844	575	1,010	738	934
Dividends: Preference	184	184	184	183	183
Ordinary	458	392	540	524	524
Profit Retained	202	(1)	286	31	227
Exceptional Profits (Losses) – not included above	–	–	(98)	(450)	116
Change in Shareholders Capital	202	(1)	188	(419)	343
Ordinary Shareholders Capital	12,958	12,756	12,757	12,569	12,988
Total Capital Employed	26,029	25,770	25,592	22,180	22,300
Profit Before Tax:					
Percentage on sales	4.1	3.9	5.2	4.6	5.2
Percentage on capital employed	8.4	7.7	9.7	9.0	10.3

Note: 1966 sales figures include confectionery turnover, the confectionery division having been sold on 2 January 1967.

EXHIBIT 2   The Associated Biscuit Manufacturers Ltd and Subsidiaries

Consolidated Balance Sheets as at 31 December 1970 and 1969 (£'000)

	1970	1969
Employment of Capital		
Fixed Assets: Goodwill (from acquisition of subsidiaries)	2,654	2,654
Land, buildings, plant and machinery	14,105	13,399
Trade investments	949	1,045
	17,708	17,098
Current Assets: Stocks (lower of cost or net realisable value)	5,633	5,247
Debtors	9,695	9,888
Bank balances and deposits	861	236
	16,189	15,371
Current Liabilities: Creditors	5,092	4,379
Overdraft – UK	1,572	528
– Overseas (secured)	234	306
Taxation	741	1,323
Dividend	229	163
	7,868	6,699
Net Current Assets	8,321	8,672
Capital Employed	26,029	25,770
Represented By		
Issued Ordinary Capital of the Company (£1 shares)	3,269	3,269
Capital Reserve	1,398	1,097
Retained Profits	8,291	8,390
Attributable to the Ordinary Shareholders	12,958	12,756
4½% Cumulative Preference Shares (£1 each)	3,655	3,655
7% Cumulative Second Preference Shares (£1 each)	275	275
6% Debenture Stock (1978/83)	3,599	3,599
7¼% Debenture Stock (1990/95)	1,500	1,500
7¼% Convertible Unsecured Loan Stock (1995/98)	1,635	1,635
7¼% Debenture Stock of a subsidiary	278	318
Long term loans of subsidiaries	165	343
	7,177	7,395
Minority Interest	1,152	990
Deferred Tax	812	699
	26,029	25,770

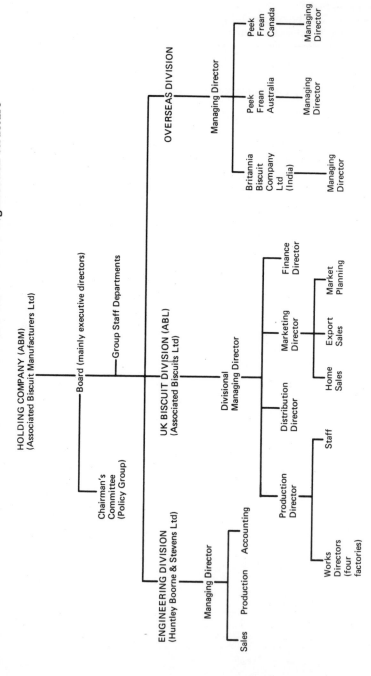

EXHIBIT 3   The Associated Biscuit Manufacturers Ltd: Organisation Structure

HOLDING COMPANY (ABM)
(Associated Biscuit Manufacturers Ltd)

Chairman's Committee (Policy Group)

Board (mainly executive directors)

Group Staff Departments

ENGINEERING DIVISION
(Huntley Boorne & Stevens Ltd)

Managing Director

- Sales
- Production
- Accounting

UK BISCUIT DIVISION (ABL)
(Associated Biscuits Ltd)

Divisional Managing Director

- Production Director
  - Works Directors (four factories)
  - Staff
- Distribution Director
- Marketing Director
  - Home Sales
  - Export Sales
  - Market Planning
- Finance Director

OVERSEAS DIVISION

Managing Director

- Britannia Biscuit Company Ltd (India)
  - Managing Director
- Peek Frean Australia
  - Managing Director
- Peek Frean Canada
  - Managing Director

10

EXHIBIT 4   The Associated Biscuit Manufacturers Ltd

Selected Companies from the Food Industry and their Profit Performance 1959–68

	Net Earnings – pence per £ Ordinary Share Capital:									
	1959	1960	1961	1962	1963	1964	1965	1966	1967	1968
ABM	38.5	27	20	19	23	8	24	23	17	24.5
Associated British Foods	25	31	34.5	36	34	41.5	46	51	48	45
Cadbury Schweppes	26.5	25.5	21.5	19	23	13	18	18	19	20.5
Imperial Tobacco	24	24	24	25	18	20.5	28.5	32.5	34	25
Lyons	–	18	12	12	12	20.5	19	13	13	16.5
Rank Hovis McDougall	16.5	18.5	18.5	17	20	20.5	27.5	21	22	28.5
Robertsons Foods	–	–	–	45	63	26	22.5	32.5	32.5	38
Rowntree Mackintosh	49	41	38	38	32.5	26.5	39	35	27.5	32.5
Wrights Biscuits	49	57	57.5	40	46	42.5	53	52	45	39
United Biscuits	28.5	31	23	26	18	17	22	20	21.5	25

Basis: 8% p.a. growth in net earnings per share from 1968

Year	A 8% growth from 1968 *Net Earnings Required Per Share £*	B *No. of £1 Ordinary Shares Generally Attributable*	B$_1$ *No. of £1 Ordinary Shares Attributable to ABL*	C A × B *Net Earnings Required for Ordinary Generally Attributable £'000's*	C$_1$ A × B$_1$ *Net Earnings Required Ordinary Attributable to ABL £'000's*
1968	0.253	3,269,567	–	827	–
1969	0.273	,,	–	893	–
1970	0.295	,,	–	965	–
1971	0.319	,,	–	1,042	–
1972	0.344	,,	–	1,125	–
1973	0.372	,,	555,900	1,216	207
1974	0.401	,,	,,	1,311	223
1975	0.434	,,	,,	1,419	241
1976	0.468	,,	,,	1,530	260
1977	0.506	,,	,,	1,654	281
1978	0.546	,,	,,	1,785	304
1979	0.590	,,	,,	1,929	328
1980	0.637	,,	,,	2,083	354

Year	I D+E+F×G+H *Net Earnings Required for Gen. Attrib. Dividends ABM Interest + Expenses*	I$_1$ C$_1$ + E$_1$ *Net Earnings Required for Dividend + Interest Attributable to ABL*	J From BBC table *Net Earnings From BBC £'000's*	K I − J *Generally Attributable Net Earnings Required From Non-Indian Sources*	L I$_1$ ÷ 0.60* *Generally Attributable Gross Earnings Required From Non-Indian Sources*
1968	1,053	56	172	881	1,450
1969	1,107	139	242	865	1,521
1970	1,165	145	249	916	1,543
1971	1,283	146	180	1,103	1,838
1972	1,383	136	182	1,201	2,002
1973	1,475	277	199	1,276	2,127
1974	1,535	293	215	1,320	2,200
1975	1,645	311	240	1,405	2,342
1976	1,759	330	261	1,498	2,497
1977	1,886	351	281	1,605	2,675
1978	2,019	374	304	1,715	2,858
1979	2,166	398	329	1,837	3,062
1980	2,323	424	356	1,967	3,278

N.B. Up to here all figures are NET of tax   ⟶   After here all figures are GROSS of tax

* ÷ 0.6074 in 1968
  ÷ 0.56875 in 1969
  ÷ 0.59375 in 1970
  ÷ 0.60 from 1971

D	E	E_1	F	G	H
C + £183					
Net Earnings Required for Generally Attributable Ordinary + Preference	Post-Tax Long-term Debt Interest Generally Attributable £'000's	Post-Tax Long-term Debt Interest Attributable to ABL £'000's	Post-Tax Short-term Debt Interest Payable by ABM £'000's	Post-Tax Short-term Debt Interest Receivable From Divisions £'000's	Post-Tax ABM Expense: £'000's
1,010	131*	56*	− 24*	94*	30*
1,076	123	139	− 10	125	43
1,148	128	145	56	220	53
1,225	130	146	102	232	58‡
1,308	130	146	144	259	60
1,399	126†	70	176	289	63
1,494	125	70	150	300	66
1,602	124	70	150	300	69
1,713	123	70	150	300	73
1,837	122	70	150	300	77
1,968	121	70	150	300	80
2,112	120	70	150	300	84
2,266	119	70	150	300	88

* Tax in 1968 at 39.26%
   in 1969 at 43.125%
   in 1970 at 40.625%
   from 1971 at 40%

† Assumed to reduce by £1,000 p.a. from here on
‡ Increasing at 5% p.a. from here

L_1	M	N	O	P	Q	R
K ÷ 0.60*				2% of o		L − M − N − Q + P
Gross Earnings Required for Dividend & Interest Attributable to ABL £'000's	Gross Royalties from a Trade Investment £'000's	Gross Dividends from a Trade Investment £'000's	Overseas Division Expenses Gross of Tax £'000's	Overseas Licensing etc. Share of Expenses £'000's	Overseas Licensing etc. Revenue Gross of Tax £'000's	Generally Attributable Gross Earnings Required from Non-Indian Subsidiaries
92	37	3	41	1	21	1,390
244	30	3	41	1	24	1,465
244	42	3	36	1	22	1,477
243	32	3	42	1	23	1,781
227	32	3	44	1	25*	1,943
462	32	3	46	1	26	2,067
488	32	3	48	1	28	2,138
518	32	4	50	1	30	2,277
550	32	4	53	1	32	2,430
585	32	4	56	1	33	2,607
623	32	4	58	1	35	2,788
663	32	4	61	1	38	2,989
707	32	4	64	1	40	3,203

* Hereafter assumed to increase at 6% p.a.

S	T	U	V	W	X
+ 23.1% of 0	23.1% of 0	* (ABL% of R) + L_1	* H.B. & S.% of R	* IMP% of R	* PF (C)% of R
PF (C) Share of Overseas Gross Expenses £'000's	PF (A) Share of Overseas Gross Expenses £'000's	Gross Earnings required from ABL £'000's	Gross Earnings required from H.B. & S. £'000's	Gross Earnings required from Pinart £'000's	Gross Earnings required from PF (C) £'000's
9	9	1,230	74	2	115
9	9	1,408	103	2	111
8	8	1,439	95	2	112
10	10	1,686	115	2	135
10	10	1,841	128	2	157
11	11	2,179	136	2	160
11	11	2,264	141	3	166
12	12	2,410	150	3	176
12	12	2,569	160	3	188
13	13	2,751	172	3	202
13	13	2,939	184	3	216
14	14	3,146	197	4	232
15	15	3,368	211	4	248

* For these percentages, which are different for 1968, 1969, 1970 and 1972 onwards, see note 9.

Notes to Exhibit 5

1. The £1.5 million of 7¾ per cent debenture stock and £1.635 million of 7¾ per cent convertible unsecured loan stock had been issued expressly to finance the modernisation programme of the UK Biscuit Division, ABL. Accordingly, the interest burden, and subsequent required earnings on the additional shares when conversion is assumed to have taken place, on these securities was considered to be part of the earnings stream of ABL rather than being included in the calculation of the profit objectives of the Group's operating units as a whole.

2. The post-tax long-term debt interest generally attributable was the interest on the £3.599 million of 6 per cent debenture stock. The interest charges on the other small portions of long-term debt were simply treated as a charge against the particular operating units who had issued that debt, a charge borne against their earnings flows before arriving at a profit objective for these units.

3. ABM charged the divisions interest on any funds they employed above a specified funds base which had been established for each division. Interest received from the divisions was offset against the overall interest burden of the Group. These interest charges on the divisions were subsumed into divisional profit objectives as charges against their earnings flows; i.e. profit objectives were set before tax but after interest payable to Group.

4. Post-tax ABM expenses referred to Head Office costs.

5. BBC stands for The Britannia Biscuit Company Limited, ABM's 53 per cent owned Indian subsidiary. Because of the minority ownership in this company and special circumstances surrounding its operations it was treated separately in the derivation of profit objectives and then subsequently incorporated into the Group planning of profit targets as shown in the exhibit.

6. Overseas Division expenses were incurred by the divisional management at company headquarters.

7. Licensing revenue arose from agreements between ABM and companies in New Zealand, Thailand, France and Italy.

8. PF (C) and PF (A) refer to Peek Frean (Canada) Ltd and Peek Frean (Australia) Ltd, the company's subsidiaries in these countries.

Y	Z	AA	BB	
X + S	* PF (A)% of R	Z + T	$\dfrac{J}{0.60}*+P+Q+X+Z$	
Gross Earnings Required from PF (C) Incl. Expenses £'000's	Gross Earnings Required from PF (A) £'000's	Gross Earnings required from PF (A) Incl. Expenses £'000's	Gross Earnings required from Overseas Div. After Expenses £'000's	Year
124	68	77	486	1968
120	77	86	636	1969
120	78	86	630	1970
145	94	104	551	1971
161	105	115	583	1972
171	111	122	628	1973
177	115	126	666	1974
188	123	135	728	1975
200	131	143	785	1976
215	141	154	853	1977
229	150	163	907	1978
246	161	175	978	1979
263	173	188	1,053	1980

* 0.6074 in 1968
0.56875 in 1969
0.59375 in 1970
0.60 from 1971

9. In arriving at the profit objectives of the various operating units, the percentages applied to the generally attributable gross earnings required from non-Indian subsidiaries were in proportion to the capital employed by the units expressed as a percentage of total capital employed. The percentages were then corrected to allow for actual rates of tax applying to overseas companies.

EXHIBIT 6   The Associated Biscuit Manufacturers Ltd

ABL Divisional Objectives

	A Profit objective	B 9% on capital employed	C Difference between 9% and 1975 profit objective (£2412)	D Dual Objective (A + C)	Actual
1968	1230	2120	negative	1230	1386
1969	1408	2254	negative	1408	1181
1970	1439	2382	negative	1439	1014
1971	1686	2493	81	1767	
1972	1841	2592	180	2021	
1973	2179	2655	243	2422	
1974	2264	2700	290	2552	
1975	2412	2745	333	2743	

EXHIBIT 7   The Associated Biscuit Manufacturers Ltd

Content of Letter on Cost of Capital

C. B. Barber, Esq.,
Group Finance Director,
The Associated Biscuit Manufacturers Ltd.,
READING

Dear Mr. Barber,

Now that you have furnished me with the particulars of your new Debenture and Loan Stock issue, I have done some cost of capital calculations on the basis of these and the data which you gave me previously.

The main points to note are as follows:

1) I have assumed a dividend cover of 2.0 on average when calculating the cost to ABM of equity finance.

2) The cost of capital depends upon your decision about the rate of return required by ABM shareholders.

3) My definition of gearing is in terms of income magnification, rather than asset structure. I therefore refer below to gearing of 65.2 per cent, taking

$$\text{Gearing} \quad \frac{\text{Debentures} + \text{Loan Stock} + \text{Preference Shares}}{\text{Total Funds}}$$

4) The cost of capital will change in 1973 / 5 when conversion of Loan Stock into Equity takes place. However, I assume you will issue additional debt finance during this period, thereby preventing the cost of capital from rising abruptly.

The calculation for the cost of capital is laid out below. The cost of each form of finance is given net, after taxation.

A. B. M. Weighted Average Cost of Finance
(after 1968 issues)

	Amount (£'000)	%of Total Funds	Percentage Cost	Weighted Cost
Ordinary Shares & Reserves	5,724	34.8	12.0*	4.17*
4½ per cent Cum. Preference	3,655	22.2	4.5	0.99
7 per cent Cum. Preference	275	1.6	7.0	0.11
6 per cent Debentures	3,680	22.4	3.5	0.78
7¾ per cent Debentures	1,500	9.1	4.6	0.41
7¼ per cent Covn. Loan Stock	1,635	9.9	4.6	0.45
	16,469	100.0	W.A.C.C.	= 6.91*

*These figures arise on the basis that Ordinary Shareholders are assumed to require a rate of return in money terms, but net of all personal taxation of 9 per cent. This is the average performance of a sample of UK Equities from 1919–1966.

There are, however, good reasons for neglecting this figure. Essentially these are:

a) A. B. M. now has a financial structure which results in income gearing of 65.2 per cent. This is extremely high for UK companies, even when their income stream is very stable.

b) A. B. M. earnings have been fairly unstable over the past six years:

Year:	1962	1963	1964	1965	1966	1967
A. B. M. interest in:			£'000			
Profit after tax:	738	870	866	425	970	738

Given the apparent ABM policy of maintaining a constant rate of dividend (currently at 16 per cent per annum) this produces an unreliable stream of retained earnings, which should bring about fluctuations in Ordinary Share prices as well as making future capital budgeting difficult.

Taken in combination, I would suggest that the rate of return which would be required by investors on the open market for shares with equivalent risks to those of ABM would be well in excess of the 9 per cent quoted above.

This suggestion is backed by the concentration of ABM activity in one industry. In the light of these considerations, a required rate of return of 15 per cent or 16 per cent would seem a fairer assumption. (Note that the average discounted rate of return on ICI shares over the past 20 years has been in excess of 13 per cent for substantially lower gearing and higher levels of company diversification.)

Recalculating on these assumptions, we obtain the following:

Shareholders' Required Rate of Return	Cost of Equity Finance	Weighted Average Cost of Capital
15%	19.5%	9.51%
16%	20.8%	9.97%

My own suggestion is that the use of a discount rate of 10% for calculating Net Present Values would not be too far off the mark.

Yours sincerely,

(*signed*) Professor C. N. Ziemer

2 BCM (Industrial Holdings) Ltd

The BCM group was a major supplier of materials to the building and construction industries. In 1968 the group's turnover exceeded £50 million; approximately half of this amount was derived from foreign markets. Net assets (fixed assets plus working capital) of the group at the end of 1968 and net profit for that year were £60 million and £3.5 million respectively.

Organisation and Management

The company was organised into several product divisions. Divisional managements had a large degree of autonomy for decisions concerning the operations of their respective divisions. A small headquarters staff was responsible for the firm's overall strategy, which included the approval and authorisation of all decisions concerning financing and capital investments, for providing specialised services such as legal and tax counsel, and for reviewing performance of the operating divisions.

Financial Measurement of Performance

A measure called 'rate of return on divisional assets' was used in evaluating the overall financial performance of the divisions. This was computed by dividing a division's after-tax profits for a year by the net book value of its assets at the beginning of the year. Financing costs, and expenses incurred by the headquarters staff, were not charged to the operating divisions when calculating divisional profits; cash, and short-term investments of cash, were not included in a division's asset base.

BCM used as a financial objective a worldwide rate of return on capital employed of 10 per cent. In the capital budgeting process, 10 per cent was used as a discount rate; proposed capital expenditures were normally required to show a positive net present value if they were to be given further consideration.

The Cement Division

One of the company's divisions was engaged in the manufacture and sale of cement. The division operated a number of cement plants in Britain, and it had a wholly-owned subsidiary in each of the following countries: Canada, Australia, Argentina, Colombia, France, Italy and West Germany. Each of the foreign subsidiaries operated one plant and sold its production within its national market.

Divisional management appraised the financial performance of domestic and foreign operations using somewhat different measures for each. Operating profit from manufacture and sale of cement in the U.K. was charged with divisional overhead expenses, which included expenses for activities such as product development and central marketing services. The resulting net profit (after provision for income tax) was divided by the net book value of the investment in plant, property, equipment, inventories and trade receivables to arrive at a 'rate of return for domestic operations'. The foreign subsidiaries were appraised on the basis of a ratio, the numerator of which was called 'net profit to BCM Ltd'. The computation of the measure of performance for

---

The name of the company involved, the industry, and the figures in the case have all been disguised.

a subsidiary is demonstrated in the example below:

BCM GmbH: Financial Performance – Fiscal Year 1968

Net Profit – after local taxation		£285,000
Management and technical fees due to BCM Ltd.	£165,000	
Less: U.K. tax on fee income	65,000	100,000
Interest due to BCM Ltd. on loans	£ 12,500	
Less: U.K. tax on interest income	5,000	7,500
Interest on local borrowing[1]	£ 15,000	
Less: local tax	7,500	7,500
Net Profit to BCM Ltd.		£400,000
Asset Base at beginning of year[2]		£3,320,000
RETURN ON ASSETS		12.0%

[1] Net of income from short-term investments of cash
[2] Net book value of assets, less cash and short-term investments of cash

The financial director of the Cement Division, discussing the financial measure of performance used for the subsidiaries, commented that he was considering changing the measure to a before-tax basis on the grounds that tax rates varied considerably from country to country, and moreover that the tax rate in a country was not a factor which could be controlled by a subsidiary manager.

3 Bultman Automobiles, Inc.

William Bultman, the part-owner and manager of an automobile dealership, felt the problems associated with the rapid growth of his business were becoming too great for him to handle alone. (See Exhibit 1 for current financial statements.) The reputation he had established in the community led him to believe that the recent growth in his business would continue. His long-standing policy of emphasising new car sales as the principal business of the dealership had paid off, in Mr Bultman's opinion. This, combined with close attention to customer relations so that a substantial amount of repeat business was available, had increased the company's sales to a new high level. Therefore, he wanted to make organisational changes to cope with the new situation. Mr Bultman's three 'silent partners' agreed to this decision.

Accordingly, Mr Bultman divided up the business into three departments: a new car sales department, a used car sales department, and the service department. He then appointed three of his most trusted employees managers of the new departments: John Ward was named manager of new car sales, Marty Ziegel was appointed manager of used car sales, and Charlie Lassen placed in charge of the service department. All of these men had been with the dealership for several years.

Each of the managers was told to run his department as if it were an independent business. In order to give the new managers an incentive, their remuneration was calculated as a straight percentage of their department's gross profit.

Soon after taking over as the manager of the new car sales department, John Ward had to settle upon the amount to offer a particular customer who wanted to trade his old car as part of the purchase price of a new one with a list price of $3600. Before closing the sale, Mr Ward had to decide the amount of discount from list he would offer the customer and the trade-in value of the old car. He knew he could deduct 15 per cent from the list price of the new car without seriously hurting his profit margin. However, he also wanted to make sure that he did not lose out on the trade-in.

During his conversations with the customer, it had become apparent that the customer had an inflated view of the worth of his old car, a far from uncommon event. In this case, it probably meant that Mr Ward had to be prepared to make some sacrifices to close the sale. The new car had been in stock for some time, and the model was not selling very well, so he was rather anxious to make the sale if this could be done profitably.

In order to establish the trade-in value of the car, the manager of the used car department, Mr Ziegel, accompanied Mr Ward and the customer out to the parking lot to examine the car. In the course of his appraisal, Mr Ziegel estimated the car would require reconditioning work costing about $200, after which the car would retail for about $1050. On a wholesale basis, he could either buy or sell such a car, after reconditioning, for about $900. The wholesale price of a car was subject to much greater fluctuation than the retail price, depending on colour, trim, model, etc. Fortunately, the car being traded-in was a very popular shade. The retail automobile dealers handbook of used car prices, the 'Blue Book', gave a cash buying price range of $775 to $825 for the trade-in model in good condition. This range represented the distribution of cash prices paid by automobile dealers for that model of car in the area in the past week. Mr Ziegel estimated that he could get about $625 for the car 'as-is' (that is, without any work being done to it) at next week's auction.

The new car department manager had the right to buy any trade-in at any price he thought appropriate, but then it was his responsibility to dispose of the car. He had the alternative of either trying to persuade the used car manager to take over the car and accepting the used car manager's appraisal price, or he himself could sell the car through wholesale channels. Whatever course Mr Ward adopted, it was his primary responsibility to make a profit for the dealership on the new cars he sold, without affecting his performance through excessive allowances on trade-ins. This primary goal, Mr Ward said, had to be 'balanced against the need to satisfy the customers and move the new cars out of inventory—and there was only a narrow line between allowing enough on the used car and allowing too much.'

After weighing all these factors, with particular emphasis on the personality of the customer, Mr Ward decided he would allow $1200 for the used car, provided the customer agreed to pay the list price for the new car. After a certain amount of haggling, during which the customer came down from a higher figure and Ward came up from a lower one, the $1200 allowance was agreed upon. The necessary papers were signed, and the customer drove off.

Mr Ward returned to the office and explained the situation to Ronald Bradley, who had recently joined the dealership as accountant. After listening with interest to Mr Ward's explanation of the sale, Mr Bradley set about recording the sale in the accounting records of the business. As soon as he saw the new car had been purchased from the manufacturer for $2500, he was uncertain as to the value he should place on the trade-in vehicle. Since the new car's list price was $3600 and it had cost $2500, Mr Bradley reasoned the gross margin on the new car sale was $1100. Yet Mr Ward had allowed $1200 for the old car, which needed $200 repairs and could be sold retail for $1050 or wholesale for $900. Did this mean that the new car sale involved a loss? Mr Bradley was not at all sure he knew the answer to this question. Also, he was uncertain about the value he should place on the used car for inventory valuation purposes.

Bradley decided that he would put down a valuation of $1200, and then await instructions from his superiors.

When Marty Ziegel, manager of the used car department, found out what Mr Bradley had done, he went to the office and stated forcefully that he would not accept $1200 as the valuation of the used car. His comment went as follows:

'My used car department has to get rid of that used car, unless John (new car department manager) agrees to take it over himself. I would certainly never have allowed the customer $1200 for that old tub. I would never have given any more than $700, which is the wholesale price less the cost of repairs. My department has to make a profit too, you know. My own income is dependent on the gross profit I show on the sale of used cars, and I will not stand for having my income hurt because John is too generous towards his customers.'

Mr Bradley replied that he had not meant to cause trouble, but had simply recorded the car at what seemed to be its cost of acquisition, because he had been taught that this was the best practice. Whatever response Mr Ziegel was about to make to this comment was cut off by the arrival of William Bultman, the general manager, and Charlie Lassen, the service department manager. Mr Bultman picked up the phone and called John Ward, the new car sales manager, asking him to come over right away.

'All right, Charlie,' said Mr. Bultman, 'now that we are all here, would you tell them what you just told me.'

Mr Lassen, who was obviously very worried, said: 'thanks Bill; the trouble is with this trade-in. John and Marty were right in thinking that the repairs they thought necessary would cost about $200. Unfortunately, they failed to notice that the rear axle is cracked, which will have to be replaced before we can sell the car. This will use up parts and labour costing about $150.

'Besides this,' Lassen continued, 'there is another thing which is bothering me a good deal more. Under the accounting system we've been using, my labour cost for internal jobs is calculated by taking the standard Blue Blook[1] price for the labour required for a

---

[1] In addition to the Blue Book for used car prices, there is a Blue Book which gives the range of charges for various classes of repair work. Like the used car book it is a weekly, and is based on the actual charges made and reported by motor repair shops in the area.

job and deducting 25 per cent. Normally, the Blue Book price is about equal to the estimated time required to do the work, multiplied by twice the mechanic's hourly rate. On parts, an outside customer pays list price, which has about a 40 per cent gross margin, but on internal work the parts are charged at cost plus 20 per cent, which is less than half the margin. As you can see from my department statement, calculating the cost of parts and labour for internal work this way didn't even cover a *pro rata* share of my department's overhead and supplies. I lost fifteen hundred bucks on internal work last year.

'So,' Lassen went on, 'on a reconditioning job like this which costs out at $350, I don't even break even. If I did work costing $350 for an outside customer, I would be able to charge him about $475 for the job. The Blue Book gives a range of $460 $490 for the work this car needs, and I have always aimed for the middle of the Blue Book range. That would give my department a gross profit of $125, and my own income is based on that gross profit. Since it looks as if a high proportion of the work of my department is going to be reconditioning of trade-ins for resale, I figure that I should be able to make the same charge for repairing a trade-in as I would get for an outside repair job. In this case, the charge would be $450.'

Messrs Ziegel and Ward both started to talk at once at this point. Mr Ziegel, the more forceful of the two, managed to edge Mr Ward out: 'This axle business is unfortunate, all right, but it is very hard to spot a cracked axle. Charlie is likely to be just as lucky the other way next time. He has to take the rough with the smooth. It is up to him to get the cars ready for me to sell.'

Mr Ward, after agreeing that the failure to spot the axle was unfortunate, added: 'This error is hardly my fault, however. Anyway, it is ridiculous that the service department should make a profit out of jobs it does for the rest of the dealership. The company can't make money when its left hand sells to its right.'

William Bultman, the general manager, was getting a little confused about the situation. He thought there was a little truth in everything that had been said, but he was not sure how much. It was evident to him that some action was called for, both to sort out the present problem and to prevent its recurrence. He instructed Mr Bradley, the accountant, to 'work out how much we are really going to make on this whole deal', and then retired to his office to consider how best to get his managers to make a profit for the company.

A week after the events described above, William Bultman was still far from sure what action to take to motivate his managers to make a profit for the business. During the week, Charlie Lassen, the service manager, had reported to him that the repairs to the used car had cost $387, of which $180 represented the cost of those repairs which had been spotted at the time of purchase, and the remaining $207 was the cost of supplying and fitting a replacement for the cracked axle. To support his own case for a higher allowance on reconditioning jobs, Lassen had looked up the duplicate invoices over the last few months, and had found other examples of the same work that had been done on the trade-in car. The amount of these invoices totalled $453, which the customers had paid without question, and the time and materials that had gone into the jobs had been costed at $335. As described by Lassen earlier, the cost figures mentioned above included an allocation of departmental overhead, but no allowance for general overhead or profit. In addition, Lassen had obtained from Mr Bradley, the accountant, the cost analysis shown in Exhibit 2. Lassen told Bultman that this was a fairly typical distribution of the service department expense.

EXHIBIT 1 Bultman Automobiles Inc.

Income Statement for the Year ended 31 December 1964

Sales of new cars			$764,375
Cost of new sales		$631,281	
Sales remuneration		32,474	
			663,755
			$100,620
Allowances on trade*			23,223
			$ 77,397
Sales of used cars		$479,138	
Appraised value of used cars	$381,455		
Sales remuneration	18,312		
		399,767	
		$ 79,371	
Allowances on trade*		12,223	
			67,148
			$144,545
Service sales to customers		$ 69,502	
Cost of work		51,397	
		$ 18,105	
Service work on reconditioning			
Charge	$ 47,316		
Cost	48,862	(1,546)	
			16,559
			$161,104
General and administrative expenses			98,342
PROFIT BEFORE TAXES			$ 62,762

* Allowances on trade represents the excess of amounts allowed on cars taken in trade over their appraised value.

EXHIBIT 2 Bultman Automobiles Inc.

Analysis of Service Department Expenses for the Year Ended December 31, 1964

	Customer Jobs	Reconditioning Jobs	Total
Number of Jobs	183	165	348
Direct labor	$ 21,386	$ 19,764	$ 41,150
Supplies	7,412	6,551	13,963
Department overhead (fixed)	6,312	5,213	11,525
	$ 35,110	$ 31,528	$ 66,638
Parts	16,287	17,334	33,621
	$ 51,397	$ 48,862	$ 100,259
Charges made for jobs to customers or other departments	69,502	47,316	116,818
Profit (loss)	$ 18,105.	($ 1,546)	$ 16,559
General overhead proportion			11,416
Departmental profit for the year			$ 5,143

4 Burmah Oil Company

In the closing months of 1975, it was by no means clear whether the chairman, Mr Alastair Down, would succeed in preventing the liquidation of the company. Mr Down was named chairman in the early part of the year after an acute liquidity crisis had brought about the departure of several top executives. The Bank of England had guaranteed certain loans to the company, but only until the end of 1975.

THE HISTORY OF BURMAH OIL BEFORE 1965

The Glasgow-based Burmah Oil Company began as a trading entity on the Indian sub-continent under the name of the Rangoon Oil Company a century ago. Its trading and exploration activities on the sub-continent were reasonably successful and continued in a worthwhile, if unexciting fashion, to the present. Around the turn of the century, however, the directors had the foresight to found the Anglo-Persian Oil Company. This company proved extremely successful. The British government took a 51 per cent shareholding in the Anglo-Persian during the First World War and the company eventually became British Petroleum. The Burmah Oil Company held 21 per cent of British Petroleum in early 1975. For similar historical reasons Burmah Oil holds $3\frac{1}{2}$ per cent of Shell Transport and Trading Company Limited.

In the 1965 consolidated profit and loss account £21.33 millions out of the total profit before tax of £27.267 millions could be attributed to dividends and interest from these holdings and others like them. The company was a major industrial holding company.

Taking the holdings in BP and Shell at market value, the investment of Burmah Oil Company represented 31 per cent of its 1965 balance sheet. But the directors were very conscious of the risks. The company was very heavily invested East of Suez. The intervention of Prime Minister Mossadecq of Iran in the operations of the Anglo-Iranian Oil Company in 1954 had made it clear that the safety of major investments in the Middle and Far East was a matter of doubt. The board decided to expand into other safer areas of the world and developed a series of oil exploration activities in Australia, Canada, New Zealand, Peru and Equador. All of these developments were in oil or closely related businesses.

THE INDUSTRIAL EXPANSION PERIOD, 1966–72

In 1965 the Board recognised that the company had to take specific action. In a document published in February 1973 entitled 'Special Report to Stockholders' the board of directors pointed out that the earnings of 1965 activities were inevitably in a state of decline. It was particularly felt that remittable earnings from India, Pakistan, Equador and Peru would decline sharply over the period ended 1971.

Burmah could not generate much cash after taxes at its international headquarters, so that it could not engage in the kind of major exploration which significant oil companies are expected to perform. In addition, since the company had only dividend income of any scale, it was unable to charge the costs of exploration against earnings for tax purposes. The board of directors of Burmah Oil Company, in other words, found themselves in the frustrating position of possessing £250 million or more in assets, but being quite unable to obtain the kinds of benefits which such a capital sum ought to bring with it. Accordingly, they decided to diversify in a fashion which would reverse the decline of operational earnings and also increase the proportion of these operational earnings relative to the dividends received from BP.

They decided they would make full use of the financial strength of the company in this objective and would increase the spread and reduce the intensity of risk by concentrating on new investment in those areas which were expected to enjoy political and monetary stability, and economic growth. They also decided to try to avoid any direct confrontations with the major oil companies and to keep out of the Middle East in view of their already significant position there through BP.

In implementing this objective the Burmah board of directors knew that they had bought, in Lobitos, a small but effective lubricating oil refining and marketing company active in South America as well as the U.K. They decided to move into this area in a larger way by acquiring Castrol, the largest company in the U.K. lubricants market. With Castrol, the company also obtained a significant leadership position in many other countries. Burmah Oil issued 6.4 million ordinary shares and £21.2 million in loan stock (7½ per cent) in consummating this merger. In the 1966 balance sheet, the tax advantage of the acquisition of Castrol in providing some UK-based earnings was again emphasised. The relationship between the activities of Castrol and the existing operations of the group was widely appreciated at the time of the acquisition and the merger seemed to be a successful one. But there was very little left in the oil business in Britain that Burmah could acquire – the industry was nearly all owned by the major British and American oil companies.

The company started to look outside the oil business for further acquisitions. In acquiring Lobitos and Castrol, Burmah had also acquired a number of subsidiary companies in such industries as building materials; mechanical seals; petroleum plant construction and electrical saturants. The board of directors decided that they would attempt to make acquisitions in fields already touched upon by their portfolios of subsidiaries. They decided to purchase the market leader in each case of the industry in which the Lobitos and Castrol subsidiaries had been operating prior to their acquisition.

They bought Rawlplug to strengthen their presence in the building industry, and Halfords to strengthen the retail side of their presence in the motoring market. They also added Quinton Hazell, a major distributor of silencers and other vehicle components. The company reported that by 1971 the capital employed and the net profit before interest, taxes, and extraordinary items relating to Castrol, Rawlplug and Halfords had been as shown in the table.

	Average Capital Employed £ millions	New Pre-Tax Profit £ millions
Castrol	64.6	9.1
Rawlplug	26.3	1.0
Halfords	16.7	2.0

These were not the only acquisitions which the company had attempted to make. They tried, without success, to purchase Laporte Chemicals, at that time the first largest chemical company in the U.K. They also attempted to develop an association with the Continental Oil Company of the United States, a relationship which proved difficult because of the American anti-trust regulations. The American government became suspisious of the relationship which would exist in the American domestic market between Conoco and Sohio because of the former's proposed tie-up with Burmah's stock-holding in BP and BP's financial relationships with Sohio. The relationships may have been tenuous but in any event the merger didn't happen.

STOCKHOLDERS' CONCERN ABOUT PROBLEM AREAS

As already indicated, Lobitos had been engaged in refining South American oil for many years. These refining activities took place in two small refineries in Manchester and at Ellesmere Port. After the acquisition of Castrol, it was decided to expand the Ellesmere Port refinery so that it could process Middle East crude oil as well as the South American, and thereby ensure adequate supplies to Castrol to help meet its expanding delivery requirements. Although the cost of this expansion was originally estimated in May 1967 at £12 million, the investment was steadily increased until a figure of £41 million was included in the special report to stockholders in February 1973, as already mentioned. A variety of factors, including strikes, underestimation and changes to the plans were blamed for this significant adjustment in capital cost.

This refinery difficulty and a sense of uncertainty about the general strategy adopted by Burmah Oil led to considerable discontent on the part of some of Burmah Oil's stockholders. The discontent arose because the expansion in turnover and in capital employed did not seem to be having very much effect in terms of earnings per share growth. Between 1967 and 1971 turnover grew from £151 million to £356 million (136 per cent growth). In the same time period the total funds employed by the group grew from £446 million to £749 million (68 per cent increase). But in total earnings grew only by 10 per cent in the five-year period. And total earnings per share grew from 20.7 pence to 20.9 pence, only a 1 per cent growth during a period of reasonable prosperity for most industries.

Two of the most discontented stockholders were Denis Blake and William Dawkins. Mr Blake had the most important shareholding in Standard Tyre Company. This firm was taken over by Quinton Hazell in 1972, very shortly before Hazell was in turn taken over by Burmah Oil Company. Indeed it was the decline in Quentin Hazell's stock price brought about by the Standard Tyre Company bid which made the takeover of Hazell by Burmah appear financially feasible.

Blake and Dawkins pointed out that the quoted shares held by Burmah Oil in British Petroleum, Shell and Woodside-Burmah (an Australian exploration company in which Burmah has a 54 per cent stake) were worth (in November 1972) approximately £600 millions. This was very approximately the value of the entire market capitalisation of the Burmah Oil Company. Accordingly, they contended that since Castrol, Rawplug, Halfords, Quentin Hazell and the operating units of the Burmah Oil Company were clearly worth something, the entire corporation could profitably be subdivided, leaving the Burmah stockholders much better off. Although the board of directors successfully fought off the challenge of Blake and Dawkins they did concede the necessity of informing the stockholders in more detail of what they were doing. The special report to stockholders of February 1973 was the most tangible consequence of the 'stockholders' revolt.'

DEVELOPMENTS IN THE OIL TANKER MARKET

Early in 1973 the company began an ambitious programme of investment in oil tankers as its contribution to the solution of the American energy gap. At that time the growth in demand for oil in the United States was estimated to average a million barrels a day per year over the decade to come. It looked as if at least a third of America's energy needs would have to be imported by 1980.

The American conservation movement had very successfully resisted the construction of major terminal facilities on the American mainland. The possibility of a very large crude carrier floundering off the American coast and spilling half a million tons of oil on to the beach was politically daunting. The conservationists were also concerned about the composition of the oil being imported. Middle Eastern oil with a relatively high sulphur content was less attractive than African oil for this reason.

At the same time the American labour movement was concerned to ensure that if oil did have to be brought, it would be brought in ships built by American labour. The American government arranged to provide a 41 per cent building subsidy provided the ship was built and registered in the United States. This subsidy more or less cancels out the additional costs (largely through higher labour charges) of building in the United States rather than in Europe.

The Burmah Oil system for moving the crude from the Middle East to the United States was similar in most respects to the concepts used in other oil companies. A transhipment terminal with very deep water access was planned for the Bahamas. A fleet of 12 super-tankers capable of carrying 350,000 tons apiece would bring the crude oil to the Bahamas terminal. Another fleet of a dozen smaller (80,000-ton) ships would carry the oil the rest of the way to the Eastern coast of the U.S.

This strategy obviously involves very substantial financing operations. In most cases Burmah took the vessels on a long-term charter basis from specially created financing corporations based in the United States. The contractual commitment payable during 1974 was reported at £53 million in the 1973 annual report. The commitments for 1975 were £63 million. The present value of the remaining contractual commitments extending up to the year 2003 was given in that annual report at £313 million. This corresponds to £48 million per annum or a total of £1341 million.

These commitments are not at all abnormal in the oil tanker chartering business. All large oil companies must make provision for the transhipment of their product. However, most of the larger oil companies simply work out how many ships they will need and buy (or charter) sufficient to meet their own anticipated requirements. They do not go into the short-term chartering of these vessels except where essential to meet short-term fluctuations in demand. Naturally, the capital involved is great and the time periods are so long that it is difficult to do these calculations correctly in an inflationary period. None the less, if the estimates are done reasonably well the worst that can happen to such a shipping company would be that it would be forced to release a small part of its fleet to cover operating losses.

But there is another way in which the oil company can choose to obtain revenues from their shipping activities. Burmah Oil, almost alone amongst the significant oil companies, chose to enter the short-term tanker chartering market.

The short-term chartering arrangement depends very much on current views of the market and short-term demand. Since the bulk of the crude oil is shipped in carriers owned and operated by the oil companies themselves, it is only the marginal demand which is required for short-term chartering purposes. This means that the price at which short-term charters can be arranged is subject to very considerable fluctuations. The index of short-term chartering prices is known as the 'World Scale'. This index moved from 100 in early 1973 to 300 in September 1973 to 95 in November 1973, and stood at 35 in December 1974. As the short-term chartering trade was extremely profitable during 1973, a large number of new vessels were ordered during the boom period. The short-term market collapsed in the summer of 1974, so there was an acute over-supply of tanker capacity in early 1975. No early recovery from the present low level seemed likely. It has been estimated that the break-even point for operating tankers is in the region of World Scale 75.

Mr Kulukundis, who was in charge of the Burmah Tanker Company, had 25 vessels under the short-term tanker market system in early 1973. It was intended that they would be put on to a long-term charter to a Middle Eastern government in early 1974. This government was interested in moving 'down stream' into the transhipment and petrochemicals sectors of the petroleum market. Unfortunately this long-term chartering arrangement did not materialise. Burmah Oil Company's vessels became surplus to world requirements.

THE SIGNAL OIL AND GAS COMPANY ACQUISITION

On March 11 1974 the stockholders of Burmah Oil Company received a letter from Mr Lumsden intimating the acquisition of Signal Oil and Gas Company and advising them that the acquisition price was $420 million in cash. The company arranged with the Orion Bank Limited and the Chase Manhattan Bank for loans to be provided. $270 million were borrowed domestically in the United States and the rest in Eurodollars. The rate of interest applicable to the U.S. borrowing was 10.6 per cent and the Eurodollar borrowing 9 per cent. The loan had a maximum life of 10 years. Mr Lumsden was chairman until February 1975.

The acquisition of Signal Oil Company was intended to ensure that the company would have sufficient reserves of crude oil and natural gas in politically stable and economically growing areas. The Signal Company held reserves producing 50,000 barrels of oil per day and a 100 million cubic feet of gas. This addition would approximately double Burmah Group oil production and would reduce the Indian/ Pakistan proportion to about a quarter.

The total reserves of the company were estimated at 223 million barrels of oil and 363 billion cubic feet of gas. In addition the company held a 19 per cent direct interest in the Thistle Oil Field in the North Sea, in which production was expected to begin in 1977. It was expected that this field would be capable of producing 100,000 barrels of oil per day but that a total cost of developing the field of approximately £13 million would have to be invested. The total assets of Signal Oil were estimated by the Burmah directors as follows:

	$ millions
Fixed assets	400
Investments and long-term receivables	51
Net current assets	(3)
Long term debt	(28)
Totals	420

The income of the Signal Oil Company before tax has been as follows:

1971	$ 39 million
1972	$ 38 million
1973	$ 53 million

THE LIQUIDITY CRISIS

The funds needed to buy Signal Oil were substantial, and Burmah had used its holding in BP to guarantee the loans. In the 1973 report it was stated that the holding was worth more than £433 million. By the end of 1974, this figure had dropped to £174 millions, and in the process had fallen below the limits required by the loan agreement.

A renegotiation of the loan took place in late 1974, but the new terms required the company to attain a certain level of profit. It became obvious, almost at once, that the tanker problem was going to make the required level of profit unobtainable.

The company then issued a statement which speaks for itself:

'Since the interim announcement in September there has been a sharp downward revision of the anticipated results for 1974, largely due to the tanker operations which are now expected to show a substantial loss. On the information at present available to them, the Board believes that the Group's results for the full year may disclose a small profit. The interim dividend already declared will be paid in January, but no further Ordinary dividend for 1974 can be expected.

'As a result of the anticipated trading results for the year, the Company expects that it will not be able fully to comply with certain provisions of loan agreements with bankers under which foreign currency loans amounting to $650 million have been advanced to the Group in connection with its overseas activities. In addition as a result of the substantial fall in the market value of its investments in the British Petroleum Company Limited the Company will be entering into discussions with the Trustees of its £54m 8½ per cent Unsecured Loan Stock 1991/96.

'Following discussions with H. M. Government and the Bank of England, the following arrangements have been agreed between the Company and the Bank of England to provide interim support to the Company pending realization of certain major assets in continuation of a programme already in hand.

1. It is proposed that certain existing long-term dollar borrowings amounting to $650m will be re-negotiated as 12 month borrowings guaranteed by the Bank of England.

2. In addition, the Bank of England has offered certain assistance to enable the Company to deal with its sterling borrowings.

3. Certain changes will be made in the management of the Company.

4. Messrs. Peat, Marwick, Mitchell and Co. will be appointed to assist in the financial management of the Group.

5. A full review of the tanker operations will be undertaken in the light of the independent investigation already commissioned by the Company early in December.

'As security for the assistance provided the Company's unpledged holdings of shares of the British Petroleum Company Limited and the 'Shell' Transport and Trading Company Limited will be made over to the Bank of England with the right of realization.

'After completing these dispositions, the Company will continue to own substantial interests in the United Kingdom and overseas. The Company will pursue the development of its important North Sea interests, in particular in the Ninian and Thistle fields. In addition it has accepted the principle of 51 per cent public participation in their share of these fields.

'The Council of the Stock Exchange in London has, at the request of the Company, agreed to suspend the listing of all the securities of the Company for the time being.

A copy of this announcement will be sent to all holders of the Company's registered securities.'

On 2 January 1975 the company made a further statement: 'Arising from certain comments on radio and television relative to the announcement made on December 31 the Company feels it necessary to clarify the following points:

1. The Group continues to trade normally.

2. Reference to the fact that the Company might not be able fully to comply with certain provisions of foreign currency loan agreements is related specifically to aspects of the covenants and ratios associated with such agreements and does not in any way imply inability on the part of the Company to pay due amounts either of principal or interest.

3. The Company's holding of 21.6 per cent of the shares of the British Petroleum Company Limited has not been taken over either by the Government or the Bank of England but has been pledged to the Bank of England as collateral in return for the assistance provided, the Bank being given the right of realization.

4. The Company has in no sense 'given away' to the Government 51 per cent of its interests in the Ninian and Thistle Fields in the North Sea. The Government has already announced its intention to seek to negotiate a 51 per cent participation in all North Sea fields. Burmah has accepted that the Government should acquire 51 per cent of its own interests in the North Sea. The precise terms of the Government's participation remain to be negotiated.'

1975 ACTIVITIES

In the first few weeks of the year, the liquidity of the firm continued to deteriorate. The board became uncertain whether the company should continue to trade or should go into liquidation. Eventually, they decided to sell the company holding in BP to the Bank of England to cover some immediate needs. The Bank then took an immediate security over other assets of the company, especially the Signal Oil shares, to cover the loans it had guaranteed.

The bank paid 230p for each share, which turned out to be the lowest price for which BP shares traded in any volume. The price was up to 380p by April.

In February, Mr A. Downs took office, and most of the old directors resigned. A few were retained 'for continuity'. Mr Downs announced his priorities in a letter to the shareholders in February 1975. They were

1. To raise funds to pay off $650 million in loans;
2. To tackle the tanker problem;
3. To continue to develop the Ninian and Thistle fields in the North Sea; and
4. To continue to develop the group's trading.

He got off to a quick start. By the end of February he had sold Great Plains Development Company of Canada for $Can 96 million. This had been purchased the year before for a slightly smaller sum.

But by September, when the half-year figures came out, not much else had been achieved. The company lost £11 million in the half, though the Great Plains profit reduced the deficit to £6.25 millions. A revenue increase of 8½ per cent was not enough to offset a £17.9 million loss on the tanker operation.

One of the difficulties was the need to keep on with the development of the North American assets, especially Signal Oil, in order to keep these assets in a condition that might interest a buyer. Also the company had to find £300 million more to finance its share of the North Sea.

QUESTIONS FOR DISCUSSION

(1) Analyse the events that led to the 1974 liquidity crisis. Were they strategic errors, financing errors, or just plain bad luck? How, if at all, could the crisis have been avoided?
(2) Could a shareholder have predicted the problems at any time prior to December 1974? If so, how?
(3) What should Mr. Downs do next?
(4) Comment on the company's disclosure practices, taking into account the letter describing the Signal Oil purchase. Do the 1973 accounts show a 'true and fair view' of the enterprise? Exhibit 2 is the five year summary section of the 1973 report, while Exhibit 3 is a transcript of two notes to these accounts. Exhibit 1 summarises the financial transactions of 1973–4.

EXHIBIT 1

	1973 Balance Sheet	Income Statement	Signal Oil Purchase	Revaluations	Other Investments	1974 Balance Sheet
Preference Capital	190					190
Ordinary Capital	1439			1		1440
Share Premium	300		3			303
Capital Surplus	366		14			380
Investment Reval.	3725			2718		1007
General Retention	945	154		101		690
Goodwill	730		156			886
Minority	421	351		420		352
Loan Capital	1291		2089		1490	4870
Deferred Liabilities	975			625		350
Properties and Op.	3037	773	1740		191	5354
Invest. Assoc.	347	387			16	363
Trade	503		220	263		460
BP	4429			2602		1827
Tankers	91			17		74
Bank	32				6	24
Current Assets	2717		1339		1289	4056
Current Liabilities	2234	189	1349	981		3462
	11886	927	3455	3864	1496	13044
	11886	927	3455	3864	1469	13044

EXHIBIT 2 Five Year Summary
The Burmah group

Group balance sheet

	1969	1970	1971	1972	1973
					£ millions
Employment of funds					
Fixed assets	98.86	128.88	161.20	218.19	303.66
Investments in associates	38.21	39.57	37.09	34.40	34.71
Trade investments/deposits	89.16	87.48	83.07	88.77	62.52
The British Petroleum Co Ltd	439.23	379.15	424.74	494.32	442.93
Current assets:					
Stores and Stocks	30.23	39.93	47.33	73.02	90.74
Debtors and prepayments	62.39	72.22	76.13	100.99	128.29
Short-term investments, bank balances and cash	65.44	42.80	31.03	27.78	52.70
	158.06	155.00	154.49	201.79	271.73
Less bank advances	24.40	24.09	35.61	63.48	97.43
Less other current liabilities	61.75	76.49	76.29	132.76	125.95
	86.15	100.58	111.90	196.24	223.38
Net current assets	71.91	54.42	42.59	5.55	48.35
	737.37	689.50	748.69	841.23	892.17
Financed by:					
Issued capital–preference	19.00	19.00	19.00	19.00	19.00
–ordinary	131.03	134.43	134.43	142.68	143.88
Reserves	461.47	408.53	452.98	505.01	460.63
Stockholders' funds	611.50	561.96	606.41	666.69	623.51
Minority interests	17.71	15.18	27.89	32.00	42.09
Loan capital	102.48	106.38	105.92	118.74	129.07
Deferred liabilities	5.68	5.98	8.47	23.80	97.50
Funds employed	737.37	689.50	748.69	841.23	892.17

	1969	1970	1971	1972	1972 Restated	1973
Sources						£ thousands
Within the group						
Earnings attributable to ordinary stockholders	25.773	27.616	28.141	30.163	21.503	44.219
Less associates' retained earnings	(725)	191	239	393	393	807
	26.498	27.425	27.902	29.770	21.110	43.412
Depreciation, depletion and amortisation	7.026	7.910	9.724	11.722	11.722	15.949
Deferred taxation	686	611	–	2.360	2.360	3.608
Proceeds from sale of assets	5.129	973	11.171	3.711	3.711	5.656
Disposals of investments	680	4.250	3.960	6.489	6.489	14.447
Certain extraordinary and prior year items			(3.293)	1.906	1.906	1.406
Miscellaneous	–	31	728	931	931	1.061
	40.019	41.200	50.192	56.889	48.229	85.539
Outside the group						
Share capital and excess on consolidation	1.169	6.635	–	32.804	32.804	5.142
Loan capital and other loans	48.726	5.334	–	13.610	13.610	53.378
Regional development and other grants	4.682	3.794	2.128	893	893	618
Finance provided by minorities and others	695	551	14.627	11.559	11.559	24.243
	55.272	16.314	16.755	58.866	58.866	83.381
	95.291	57.514	66.947	115.755	107.095	168.920
Uses						
Dividends to ordinary stockholders	21.395	21.845	21.845	13.780	13.780	15.768
Expenditure on fixed assets	33.236	45.427	52.088	75.223	75.223	93.642
Addition to investments including net advances	188	5.084	2.736	11.491	11.491	5.181
Amounts paid for goodwill	4.957	1.752	688	39.725	39.725	9.062
Repayment of loan capital	518	1.634	682	1.569	1.569	617
Miscellaneous	372	–	401	353	353	180
Increase in working capital (excluding net liquid funds)	9.724	4.565	11.797	4.732	(3.928)	53.498
	70.390	80.307	90.237	146.873	138.218	177.948
(Decrease) Increase in net liquid funds	24.901	(22.793)	(23.290)	(31.118)	(31.118)	(9.028)
	95.291	57.514	66.947	115.755	107.095	168.920

Group profit

	1969	1970	1971	1972	1972 Restated (note 1)	1973
						£ millions
Turnover net of duties	181.70	235.84	272.85	348.51	348.51	495.87
Net operating profit	13.82	15.24	19.06	26.27	26.27	48.72
Share of profits of associated companies	8.17	8.60	7.67	5.97	5.97	9.25
Dividends from UK companies (excluding dividends from BP) (note 2)	—	—	—	—	1.59	1.52
Other trade investment income	3.44	4.03	3.94	3.44	0.84	1.10
	25.43	27.87	30.67	35.68	34.67	60.59
Net interest change	2.82	5.36	7.74	9.77	9.77	16.16
	22.61	22.51	22.93	25.91	24.90	44.43
Taxation	9.56	9.99	9.43	9.41	11.16	10.40
	13.05	12.52	13.50	16.50	13.74	34.03
Minority interests etc.	2.35	1.15	1.08	1.50	1.50	1.37
Earnings attributable to ordinary stockholders (excluding dividends from BP) (notes 3 & 4)	10.70	11.37	12.42	15.00	12.24	32.66
Dividends from BP (note 1)	16.46	17.64	17.11	16.55	10.14	12.53
Preference dividends (note 1)	1.39	1.39	1.39	1.39	0.88	0.97
Dividends from BP attributable to ordinary stockholders (note 4)	15.07	16.25	15.72	15.16	9.26	11.56
Total earnings attributable to ordinary stockholders (note 3)	25.77	27.62	28.14	30.16	21.50	44.22
Ordinary dividends (note 1)	12.71	13.17	13.59	15.77	15.77	17.45
Taxation on ordinary dividends	8.92	8.68	8.59	8.66	—	—
Retained earnings	4.14	5.77	5.96	5.73	5.73	26.77
Extraordinary items			(2.36)	1.75	1.75	14.90
	4.14	5.77	3.60	7.48	7.48	41.67
Associates' retentions	(0.72)	0.19	0.06)	0.50	0.50	0.22
Group retentions	4.86	5.58	3.66	6.98	6.98	41.45
Group depreciation	7.03	7.91	9.72	11.72	11.72	15.95
Group cash flow from operations	11.89	13.49	13.38	18.70	18.70	57.40
Group capital expenditure after grants	27.50	35.47	31.10	61.93	61.93	89.96

	1969	1970	1971	1972	1972 Restated (note 1)	1973
Average capital employed (£ millions) (note 5)	312.47	328.49	347.00	384.98	384.98	478.53
Return on average capital employed	8.1%	8.5%	8.8%	9.3%	9.0%	12.7%
Ordinary stock units on which statistics have been calculated (thousands) (note 6)	131,028	134,434	134,434	141,182	141,182	143,857
Earnings attributable to ordinary stockholders (£ millions) (note 3)	25.77	27.62	28.14	30.16	21.50	44.22
Earnings per ordinary stock unit	19.67p	20.55p	20.93p	21.36p	15.23p	30.74p
Dividends per ordinary stock unit	16.25p	16.25p	16.50p	17.00p	10.9725p	12.124p
Cover for ordinary dividend based on above figures	1.21	1.26	1.27	1.26	1.39	2.54
Contribution to ordinary dividend from own operations (note 7)	4.75p	4.16p	4.81p	6.26p	4.41p	4.09p
Cover for that portion of ordinary dividend paid from own operations (note 7)	1.72	2.03	1.92	1.70	1.96	5.55
Market quotations per ordinary stock unit Highest	675p	427p	477p	496p		506p
Lowest	355p	237p	298p	363p		354p
Ordinary stockholders' equity per stock unit at year end	452p	404p	437p	454p		420p
Ratio of stockholders' funds to loan capital	86:14	84:16	85:15	85:15		83:17
Number of stockholders (thousands) Preference stocks	18.8	17.7	17.0	16.1		14.6
Ordinary stock	153.2	169.1	163.3	165.7		162.3
Loan stocks (note 8)	53.3	52.9	51.3	50.2		53.3
	225.3	239.7	231.6	232.0		230.2

Notes

1 As a result of the introduction of the new imputation tax system the figures for 1973 are not comparable with those for earlier years. However, for the purpose of comparison, the 1972 figures have been restated in a separate column. Thus in the columns for 1973 and 1972 restated, neither dividends from UK companies nor dividends payable include the related tax credits or, as appropriate, the income tax deducted at source. For 1972 and earlier years dividends are show gross.

2 Dividends from UK Companies (excluding those from BP) are included from 1969 to 1972 in other trade investment income.

3 Excluding extraordinary items.

4 As almost 80% of the preference stocks was issued in 1966 to enable Burmah to take up its share of a rights issue by BP, the total cost of the preference dividends, for the purpose of this summary, has been regarded as a charge against dividends from BP.

5 Average capital employed comprises funds employed and bank advances but excludes the investment in BP. The profit figures used are those before charging interest and taxation.

6 The ordinary stock units (a) for 1969 do not include 3,406,000 units issued in 1970 relating to the acquisition of Halfords on which final dividend for 1969 was paid and (b) for other years are based on the weighted average number of ordinary stock units in issue during each year.

7 Own operations refers to total earnings other than dividends from BP.

8 Excluding holders of foreign currency bonds.

EXHIBIT 3   Capital Expenditure of the Group

	1973 £000	1972 £000
Capital expenditure approved by the board amounts to approximately	174,000	70,000
Contracts placed against these approvals so far as not provided for in these accounts amount to approximately	9,500	6,000

In addition to the foregoing the board had approved at 31st December 1973 a cash offer of U.S. $420 million (£183 million) for all the issued equity capital of Signal Oil and Gas Company.

Commitments and Contingent Liabilities

	Group	1973 £000 Company	Group	1972 £000 Company
(a) Amounts uncalled on partly paid shares:				
Subsidiaries	–	1,122	–	901
Associates	2,261	2,261	2,250	2,250
Trade investments	276	180	281	180
	2,537	3,563	2,531	3,331
(b) Guarantees of bank overdraft facilities granted to subsidiaries	–	44,000	–	29,000
(c) Other guarantees etc.	50,000	44,000	25,500	19,500

(d) Certain subsidiaries have contractual commitments in respect of tanker incharters and leased facilities involving hire charges (exclusive of certain operating costs) as follows:

Commitments estimated as payable during 1974	£53 million
Commitments estimated as payable during 1975	£63 million
Thereafter extending up to the year 2003 there are similar commitments, the net present value of which discounted at 15 per cent per annum is estimated to amount to	£313 million

It is impossible to predict, with certainty, circumstances over a period extending beyond the year 2000 but the terms of firm out-charters, contracts of affreightment and other arrangements so far entered into, already provide for income being earned over the period to match a very substantial part of the aggregate amount of the commitments. Guarantees have been given by the company in respect of the obligations of the subsidiaries and also in relation to certain joint ventures with which they are associated. No amounts in respect of such guarantees are included in (c) at the foot of the previous column.

(e) Pensions payable under overseas social legislation and contributions to various group pension schmes.

(f) Various disputed claims for overseas taxation.

(g) Sundry commitments and contingencies arising in the ordinary course of business.

5 Cresta Plating Company Ltd

THE COMPANY BACKGROUND

Cresta Plating Company Ltd was purchased in 1946 by a group of companies to carry out the plating work of its many subsidiary companies. Cresta is one company within a division of the main group; the division being concerned predominantly with metal finishing in the widest sense. The company is located in the London area, and this was a significant factor in the decision to purchase since the majority of the companies in the group were also situated in the south east of England.

Apart from plating work for companies within the division and within the group generally, the company carries out a substantial amount of plating for companies outside the group. The proportions of work for group companies and non-group companies have recently been equal.

The company had its origins in the early 1920s and from tin-shed beginnings it expanded by the time of the purchase in 1946 to a reasonable size and had gained a sound technical reputation. All the remnants of private family business management have now disappeared. However, despite the efforts of the parent company, and a number of recent executive appointments which have been group-inspired, the 'group image' is not well established.

PRODUCTION AND PROGRESS

The company is in the electro-plating jobbing industry, and this presents problems not met in a plating shop in a factory handling work produced in that factory alone. This is an important factor, for it results in the company having limited knowledge of the orders that are coming into the factory premises. Production planning and control is extremely difficult, especially when linked to the quick delivery so vital to secure orders. The company aims at a 48-hour turnround from the receipt of an order to its despatch.

Since 1946 the company has grown rapidly and now employs about 350 people at two factories in London, one in Newcastle and another in Sheffield; the last two factories being recent acquisitions of family businesses, which although technically sound, have not been satisfactory in the financial sense.

At Cresta both barrel plating and vat plating are used. Most of the vats are hand-operated in order to achieve a flexibility necessary to cope with the different mixes of products. On the barrel plating side, there are two large automatic plants to cope with the steady flow of work from group companies. There are also a few hand-operated barrels. The company handles a wide variety of work, ranging from small orders of a few pounds weight, to huge orders where the total weight of the products involved could be as much as one ton. A wide variety of finishes is catered for, such as zinc, cadmium, tin, chromium, nickel, copper, precious metals like gold and silver, and also plastics.

The company has been profitable for a number of years and the continuation of this trend can be seen in recent results. This success has been partly due to the fact that the company has an assured market within the group. Intra-group pricing is a touchy matter within the company, and Cresta is under constant pressure to reduce transfer prices which, by the strength of its top management, it seems to withstand successfully.

Reprinted from *Management Accounting*, March 1970.

ACCOUNTING METHODS

The accounting department has a staff of 12, who cover the duties of financial accounting, cost accounting and wages for all the factories. There are, however, two clerical workers on routine accounting and wages matters, both at Newcastle and Birmingham. Until a few months ago, the only costing work being done was the recalculation of cost rates for the purpose of estimating for price-fixing. This recalculation was undertaken annually and was on an absorption costing basis. Overhead costs are categorised as fixed or variable on a basis specified by head office, and this analysis is a requirement of the trading statement prepared and submitted to head office.

The appointment was made in 1968 of a new man to the post of company secretary / chief accountant. He has proved to be quite an innovator, and one of the first tasks he undertook was to review the financial and cost accounting procedures. At one of the early board meetings he attended it was stressed that better financial controls were needed. This attitude was supported by the argument that as the company was continuing to expand, control by observation became increasingly difficult. The new man formed the impression that a certain amount of lip-service was being paid to the idea of management accounting and information services. He found that monthly and quarterly interim trading statements were being prepared, but he was disappointed that these were only total trading statements for the company. He proceeded to give immediate thought to the departmentalisation of the figures. One of the factors which weighed heavily with him was the fact that during his four week's 'acclimatisation' at head office, he had been introduced to a management by objectives programme which was in the process of being launched throughout the group. Two points that particularly impressed him about this programme were:

(a) the overall financial objective which was to be built into the programme, namely, a return on capital employed of 20 per cent before tax: and

(b) the desire to set objectives and key tasks for individual managers and executives.

This second point matched comments which had been made at the Cresta board meeting that production managers needed measures which they did not have at the moment.

BUDGETS

The accountant also had work to do on accounting returns for head office. The statements in Exhibit 1 include a budget and actual trading statement return, prepared to the group uniform pattern. The budget is an annual affair and worries the accountant somewhat, since he believes that it should have its roots in departmental budgets. This is not so at the moment, because it is produced as an overall business budget.

ACCOUNTING DEVELOPMENTS

As far as Cresta was concerned, it seemed to the accountant that departmentalisation could logically be carried to profit centres. There was vat plating, barrel plating, and there were some less significant sections; further, there were natural sub-sections in each, which were definite factory locations with directly identifiable sales. There was already in being a simple sales analysis to these profit centres. To develop the existing records into a departmental system of accounting was only a matter of arranging the necessary cost analysis procedures. These were partly in existence in a rough-and-ready fashion and were used to facilitate the task of recalculating cost rates annually. The extra work created by a full-scale cost allocation and apportionment exercise carried out each monthly accounting period was performed by two additional cost office staff specially appointed for the purpose.

There were, inevitably, some joint costs, and much thought had to be given to them, particularly on the matter of how these should be apportioned between the profit centres. In addition, there were service department costs, administration expenses and some general fixed costs, and for all of these, bases of apportionment had to be determined. It was a hard slog, but it was finally done and it was possible to produce interim profit centre trading statements.

PROFIT CENTRE TRADING STATEMENTS

The first man to see the new statements was the managing director, who took some time to warm to them, but he eventually did. The other executives were brought into a meeting to study them, and there was general agreement that they were very informative. This was the first information which top management had ever received on the profitability of different units, so that inevitably some surprise was registered about some of the figures. On this first set of departmental trading statements, the new accountant had gone no farther than to analyse sales, costs, and profits or losses. There was, however, a feeling at the meeting that the next statement should show an analysis of capital employed in profit centres in order that 'profitability' could be computed on a departmental basis. Interest was running high, and the accountant was pleased.

The next step was the analysis of capital employed, and the accountant and his staff found this analysis to profit centres was just as difficult as cost analysis. Some of the fixed capital could be identified directly with departments, but some was of a more general type. He was not at all sure about the working capital, which he felt was very much more a function of the product itself and of the customer than it was of any production department. There was also the problem of capital employed in the service departments of the company. But again, the interest in departmental profitability was something to be cultivated, and he felt that the management accounting service had an opportunity here to justify itself. The net result of all these efforts is the type of trading statement which appears in Exhibit 2.

'CAN THESE ASSESSMENTS BE RIGHT?'

The next phase in relationships between accounting and management generally at Cresta can best be described as a 'can these assessments be right?' phase. Arguments raged about the allocation and apportionment of cost to profit centres. Time and time again the accountant made the point that any allocation is arbitrary, no matter how detailed the process by which the allocation rule is determined. On the other hand, he never failed to add that each profit centre must bear its fair share of all expenses. There is no doubt that many of the management team at Cresta had been shattered by the figures. Some profit centres were shown as not so profitable as they had been thought to be. Perhaps it was natural that there were recriminations. There were comments like 'we always felt that Bert was efficient, but look how much money he's losing us'.

All this worried the accountant. Surely it was logical to have profit centre reporting? But where were the ties between profitability and efficiency, if any?

TRANSFER PRICING

Discussions between the accountant, managers and parties aggrieved by his efforts brought out many points which he felt deserved attention. The overriding one seemed to be the subject of transfer pricing. The point was made that there were inconsistencies in pricing which stemmed from two main causes; firstly, insufficient work measurement had been done to enable the establishment of reasonable standards or synthetics for estimating: and secondly, the managing director had involved himself extensively in pricing decisions. On the first point, everyone agreed that proper work measurement was difficult in this type of manufacture. Then, since it had never been seen in this factory as providing much more than a basis for wage payment, no very clear need had been established. On the second point, the managing director had been very successful in price negotiations with group companies. Using the arguments of quick turnround and quality, coupled with his prestige in the trade and his forcefulness of character, he had been able to extract advantageous prices from group companies. Clearly, this was a factor in the profitability of the various profit centres.

QUESTIONS FOR CONSIDERATION

Matters were brought to a head when the group management accountant called a meeting of executives at head office to consider a wide variety of matters, which included the profit centre reporting at Cresta. The managing director and the accountant were invited to this meeting. On the subject of the trading statements, about which the group management accountant was congratulatory, three specific points emerged for further consideration:

(a) It was agreed that the pricing of completed work was an important factor in profitability. The group management accountant recommended that the relative profitability of group work and other work should be investigated and a report produced on the subject of the pricing of inter-company transfers.

(b) The group management accountant had work to do on instituting the management by objectives programme, and one of the first factors to be determined was the rate considered to be a reasonable return on investment for Cresta. This was likely to involve some difficulties, since Cresta was already making a better rate of return or so it seemed, than the overall group requirement. Critical questions are: How is a target set in these circumstances? Does this target return apply to new capital spending?

(c) Next was the question of objectives for individual managers and whether the latter should be expected to concentrate on profitability as shown by the profit centre reports or efficiency. Consequent upon decisions being made on these matters, there was the problem of appropriate measures. At the moment, neither managers nor foremen saw any sort of detailed performance report of output, costs and efficiencies, though all managers saw the profit centre statements for the whole company. The management by objectives programme called for some means of measuring managers' performance in key results areas, and the accountant was, apparently, being called upon to play his part in this. He wondered to what extent basic budgetary control ideas might be useful in this connection, and how the performance reporting system should be designed, implemented and controlled.

The reader is invited to advise the accountant of Cresta on these three points, and also on the implications of Exhibit 2.

EXHIBIT 1 Budget and Actual Trading Statement, September 1969

	September 1969		January to September 1969	
	Budget	*Actual*	*Budget*	*Actual*
Sales: To Group Companies	£22,000	29,161	£220,000	287,103
Outside Group	38,000	27,277	380,000	285,046
	60,000	56,438	600,000	572,149
Variable Costs of Sales	35,000	32,231	350,000	335,203
Gross Margin	25,000	24,207	250,000	236,946
Other Costs				
Depreciation	2,600	2,416	26,000	24,270
Fixed Works Exes	5,200	6,637	52,000	58,643
Admin Exes	2,800	3,029	28,000	29,327
Fixed Sales Exes	2,400	1,448	24,000	20,772
	13,000	13,530	130,000	133,012
	12,000	10,677	120,000	103,934

EXHIBIT 2(a)   Profit Centre Analysis

September 1969		Totals	Barrel	Vat	H D	Spec Fin	Misc
Sales:	Group Companies	£29,161	21,625	2,604	1,445	1,877	1,610
	Others	27,277	3,630	7,564	3,457	11,426	1,200
	Totals	56,438	25,255	10,168	4,902	13,303	2,810
	Process Materials	8,271	3,599	1,885	502	1,857	428
	Direct Labour	7,140	1,374	2,003	818	2,702	243
	Indirect Labour	1,501	497	474	28	455	47
	Labour Overheads	1,296	282	366	112	497	39
	Consumables	2,308	127	470	195	857	659
	Power	4,653	1,851	452	603	1,278	469
	Maintenance	1,947	974	238	100	575	60
	Jigs	576	—	133	203	240	—
	Services	4,539	1,950	726	633	1,205	25
	Variable Costs	32,231	10,654	6,747	3,194	9,666	1,970
Gross Margin		24,207	14,601	3,421	1,708	3,637	840
Fixed Works Expenses		9,053	3,589	1,487	1,352	2,303	322
Admin and Sales Expenses		4,477	2,037	729	395	93	1,223
		13,530	5,626	2,216	1,747	2,396	1,545
Profit or (Loss)		10,677	8,975	1,205	(39)	1,241	(705)
Jan-Sept 1969							
	Sales	572,149	260,093	105,623	61,078	120,467	24,888
	Profit or Loss	103,934	77,909	8,101	4,568	9,356	4,000
	% of Sales	18.2	29.9	7.6	7.5	7.8	16.0
	Annual Rate of Profit	138,578	103,879	10,801	6,091	12,475	5,333
	Assets Employed	350,000	130,000	58,000	43,000	109,000	10,000
	ROI %	39.5	79.8	18.6	14.2	11.4	53.3

EXHIBIT 2(b)　Profit Centre Analysis

September 1969	Total Barrel	A Automatic	B Automatic	Horizontal	Chrome	Small Orders	Anodising	Spec Fin
Sales:								
Group Companies	£21,625	5,791	3,191	7,985	3,923	427	150	158
Others	3,630	247	1,926	1,177	63	217	—	—
Total	25,255	6,038	5,117	9,162	3,986	644	150	158
Process Materials	3,599	516	533	2,105	137	213	18	77
Direct Labour	1,374	282	226	474	165	112	40	75
Indirect Labour	497	65	190	150	45	39	8	—
Labour Overheads	282	50	67	94	30	25	6	10
Consumables	127	26	47	44	—	10	—	—
Power	1,851	520	568	570	118	40	15	20
Maintenance	974	65	261	375	209	64	—	—
Services	1,950	378	379	666	370	100	32	25
Variable Costs	10,654	1,902	2,271	4,478	1,074	603	119	207
Gross Margin	14,601	4,136	2,846	4,684	2,912	41	31	(49)
Fixed Works Expenses	3,589	754	1,095	1,065	465	170	20	20
Admin & Sales Expenses	2,037	486	412	738	324	52	12	13
	5,626	1,240	1,507	1,803	789	222	32	33
Profit or (Loss)	8,975	2,896	1,339	2,881	2,123	(181)	(1)	(82)
Jan-Sept 1969								
Sales	260,093	73,424	57,916	82,491	35,228	7,326	1,802	1,906
Profit or Loss	77,909	24,969	10,734	24,003	19,026	(700)	180	(303)
% of Sales	29.9	34.0	14.6	23.1	54.0	(9.7)	10.0	(16.0)
Annual Rate of Profit	103,879	33,292	14,312	32,004	25,368	(933)	240	(404)
Assets Employed	130,000	27,000	44,000	37,000	14,000	6,000	1,000	1,000
ROI %	79.8	123.3	32.5	86.5	181.2	(15.5)	24.0	(40.4)

6 The Dalgety Group

Dalgety had been growing steadily from 1971 onwards. That year was a poor one for the company, with earnings per share falling to 7.5 pence. But the growth since then had enabled an e.p.s. of 38.4 pence to be recorded in 1974. This was achieved by growth in operating profits from £3.6m to £19.15m in the four years.

In 1974, the various subsidiaries through which the company operated were reported as having differed widely in achievement. The Australian and New Zealand companies were stated, in the chairman's report, to have done relatively poorly, while the British, U.S., and Canadian units did well. The former companies were adversely affected by declining markets and very bad flooding.

J. J. Jones, partner in a medium-sized London-based investment analysis firm was trying to find out which of the subsidiaries were really doing well and which were not. The older subsidiaries were mainly in wool and beef, while the younger (Northern hemisphere) subsidiaries were diversified. In view of the importance of wool and beef to Dalgety, however, the long-term competence with which these basic commodities were managed seemed to Jones to be of crucial importance. Obviously he would have to compare performance with other companies and take other analytical steps, but at the outset he wished to work out whether the managers of the older companies in the group were doing a good job or a bad job compared to their colleagues in the new companies. Some notes on the companies are given below. Summaries of their 1976 accounts in their local currencies are given in Exhibit 1.

OPERATING COMPANIES

DALGETY U.K. LTD (G. T. Pryce)
The company had for several years been involved in pig and poultry feedstuffs. It had extended into dairy and cattle feed through two acquisitions made early in 1975. During 1974, acquisitions extended the firm's involvement in wholesale and retail foods, including frozen food centers. Malt preparation, for the brewing industry, was also important.

DALGETY AUSTRALIA LTD (W. J. Vines)
Extensive flood damage ($A1m) and extra holiday pay ($A0.7m) held back the Australian subsidiary in 1974. The high prices of beef and wool in the early part of the year helped, but a major fall in the second half in these commodities was thought likely to affect 1975 as well as the 1974 results. The company diversified out of rural products into real estate, wines and spirits, and air conditioners, which accounted for more than one third of 1974 activity. In early 1975, the company sold its wool broking and livestock operations in Western Australia, realising $A12m over a period, to concentrate on the eastern states.

DALGETY NEW ZEALAND LTD (D. C. McDougall)
The company was heavily involved in wool and cattle and was therefore hurt by the decline in prices of these items. The climate was also freakish in 1974, leaving advances to clients very high at year end.

DALGETY (U.S.A.) INC. (M. J. Weigel)
Cotton trading was hurt in 1974 by government controls, while grain trading profits quadrupled. Meat importing doubled in weight and profit. Steel importing started the

year slowly, but finished well, earning half the year's income in the last quarter. A shopping centre in California and a fish company in Seattle were also purchased. The main acquisition, for $US11m, was Spiegel Foods, a California vegetable packer selling $US27m in 'own-brand' product to supermarket chains.

BALFOUR GUTHRIE (CANADA) LTD (R. F. Owen)

The company is principally engaged in the processing of timber in British Columbia. It has grown by a factor of eight in four years. The shipping and steel operations also contributed to profits and the company's commodity traders were active especially in steel, during 1974.

SOME TECHNICAL FACTORS IN THE COMPARISON

Mr Jones was not satisfied that the accounts for the subsidiaries were sufficient information for his purposes. He felt that the problems of operating in different economies and of working with different inflation rates and variable exchange rates should be taken into consideration in assessing the relative performance of the subsidiaries within the group. The balance sheet, profit and loss account, and funds statement for the whole group are given in Exhibits 2, 3 and 4 respectively, but Mr Jones wanted more detail on each of the segments.

METHODS OF CURRENCY TRANSLATION

In the 1974 accounts, Dalgety continued the practice of translating all currencies into sterling at the rate of exchange prevailing at the balance-sheet date. The principal reason for using this method was simply stated by the President of the Institute of Chartered Accountants of Scotland, in a conversation with the casewriter. He suggested that the use of the current rate might be incorrect, but the use of some past rate was certainly wrong, as it would be a matter of pure chance whether the amounts realised upon repatriation would amount to the balance sheet figures displayed on a historic rate translation basis. If the current rate were used, the difference was still likely, but at least it would not be caused by the currency values.

The Financial Accounting Standards Board of the U.S.A., which has no jurisdiction over Dalgety, advocate the temporal method of currency translation. This implies the translation of assets at the rate in force at their acquisition date. In a note about the FASB draft opinion, Ernst & Ernst mention, as a reason for this method's adoption, that it portrays more accurately the amount of parent company currency that was originally committed to the overseas assets. The historic cost would therefore be more fairly represented by the temporal method. The FASB did not make any comment on the question of inflation adjustment in their currency exchange opinion.

An approximation to the current method is shown in Exhibit 5 and the temporal method is approximated in Exhibit 6. Neither exhibit is inflation-adjusted.

METHODS OF ACCOUNTING FOR INFLATION

In the 1974 report, the company noted that the provisional statement of standard accounting practice of the Accounting Standards Steering Committee had not been very well received by such groups as the Society of Investment Analysts. They also noted that the Sandilands report[1] had not been published at their time of writing.

---

[1] The Sandilands report was published on 4 September 1975, and advocated the use of replacement cost accounting methods for both tax and financial reporting purposes.

Accordingly, they decided not to try to report anything in the way of inflation adjusted accounts in 1974. Mr Jones was quite certain that this was not a very accurate way of comparing the companies, as he was uncomfortably aware of the high rate of inflation in the U.K. and believed that other countries had done much better.

Accordingly he set his clerk, Mr Bingley, to work to produce estimated accounts, on an inflation-adjusted basis, for all the subsidiaries, for 1974. Mr Bingley obtained a series of indices from various countries, a selection of which are reproduced in Exhibit 7. He used these to produce the acoounting reports shown in Exhibits 8, 9 and 10. He also produced a summary of the results that seemed most relevant to him, Exhibit 11. On receipt of these reports, Mr Jones called in Mr Bingley and asked for the Basis of the reports and their meanings.

'Well, Sir, let's take Exhibit 8 first,' said Mr Bingley. 'I took the accounts for each subsidiary in its local currency, and divided the assets into "new net assets" and "old net assets" as a first step. This division was an approximation, based upon the apparent age indicated from the balance sheets for June 1973 and June 1974. Then I applied the local general price level index of inflation to the numbers. The Australian results are shown in detail. For sales, for instance, I inflated the original amount by multiplying it by the end-of-financial-year index (138) and dividing it by the average value of the index for the year (131). This gave sales in June 1974-value Australian dollars.

'For expenses, I did the same thing, except that the divisor was the index value average with a six-month lag. That is, the divisor of 123 is the average of the index from the first quarter of 1973 to the last quarter of 1973. I hoped thereby to take account of the inevitable delay between a cost being incurred and its recognition as an expense.'

'Fair enough, as a first approximation, Mr Bingley,' was Mr Jones's comment. 'What about the asset translations?'

'Well, for the new assets I used the same index ratio as for sales. For the old ones I used, as the divisor, the index as it was eighteen months before the year end, that is as at December 1972,' replied Mr. Bingley. 'I wanted to try to recognise the inflation since the assets were bought, and hoped this might give us some idea of that effect.'

'Hm. Probably OK. How about this equity adjustment?', asked Mr Jones.

'In that case I simply took the equity balance at the start of the year and inflated that to the year end. 138 is the year-end index, while 120 is the year-start index,' said Mr. Bingley. 'In this instance I was trying to recognise the need to maintain the purchasing power of the equity.'

'I'm not so sure about that bit,' said Mr. Jones. 'The Institute of Chartered Accountants wants us to go through a calculation of the gain on monetary losses as well as restatement of the assets in end-of-year currency. What you have done may be the same or it may not.'

'It is very nearly the same, sir, and I hadn't the data to do their recommended procedure,' said Mr. Bingley. 'the balancing number, which I have called the inflation adjustment, is $A16782. This, together with the equity change, is a recognition of the inflation effect.

'The next step was the very simple one of translating into pounds at the 1.61 rate prevailing in June 1974. The other countries were done the same way, but I didn't show the calculations.'

'Fair enough, I see what you've done,' said Mr. Jones. 'How about the other two exhibits?'

"Exhibit 9 is the exact reverse of 8. I translated the items into pounds using the rate of exchange prevailing for each item. For the old assets, for instance, I used the rate at the end of 1972, which was 1.88. It comes out slightly less than that if you translate via the US$ as in Exhibit 7 for some reason, but that isn't important.

'The balancing number in this case is a currency adjustment, in this instance a rather large loss.'

'It surely is,' replied Mr Jones; 'it seems too high to me.'

'But the exchange rate changed by 15 per cent, sir,' said Mr Bingley, 'surely that is pretty massive and can be expected to have a big effect?'

'I suppose so,' said Mr. Jones, 'so what did you do next?'

'I just applied the inflation indices exactly as before, Mr Jones. In this instance I was using the general price index for the U.K., because we already had the translation into pounds done.'

'Right. I see that one. Now how about Exhibit 10?' asked Mr Jones.

'That is exactly the same as 8 in terms of procedure, sir, but instead of using the Australian general price index I used the special price index. I picked the wool export index, because that is their big product in Australia. I used wool export in New Zealand, import prices in U.S.A., wood pulp export prices in Canada, and the retail index in Britain,' explained Mr Bingley. 'Each of these seemed the best for its situation. Then I translated the account at its current rate of exchange.'

Mr Jones leaned back in his chair. 'I suppose you didn't do the British special price index with temporal translation, just to round out your set?'

Sarcasm was lost on Mr Bingley, 'I couldn't, sir,' he explained, 'there is no British special price index that represents all the dozens of things this group is doing.'

Mr Jones turned to Exhibit 11. He noted that Mr Bingley had left currency adjustments and inflation adjustments out of this comparative exhibit, showing only the restated sales and expense figures for each country.

'This is crazy,' he said; 'look at Canada – they have either made a 32 per cent profit or a nearly 50 per cent loss on assets, depending on the method you pick. And New Zealand makes 47 per cent by the method under which Canada loses that much. In fact the only place that is consistent is Britain and it makes a loss all the time! There must be a mistake.'

'I do not believe so, sir,' responded Mr. Bingley rather stiffly.

'No, I don't mean arithmetic, I mean errors of principle,' said Mr. Jones. 'These can't all be right – which of them is?'

'With respect, sir, you are the partner, I am just the clerk, perhaps you should tell me.'

QUESTION FOR DISCUSSION

Amongst the decisions for which a profit report may be considered one among several important and relevant factors are the decisions listed below. Which of the case exhibits best fits which decision? If none seem to fit, what steps should be taken as far as profit reporting is concerned?

1. The evaluation of the merits of the manager in charge of a subsidiary.
2. The evaluation of the performance of the subsidiary company.
3. The decision to place further corporate funds in the country in which the subsidiary is located, or to move out of that country.
4. The decision to pull out of or invest further in the industry in which the subsidiary is principally involved.
5. The decision to expand the home capital base of the Group.
6. The decision to contract the home capital base of the Group.
7. The decision to change the capital base outside the UK, either up or down.
8. The shareholders decisions to buy, hold or sell Dalgety group shares.
9. The decision to advance a loan to the Dalgety Group, by a UK bank or other financial institution.
10. The decision to advance a loan to a subsidiary by a financial institution in that subsidiary's nation.

EXHIBIT 1 THE DALGETY GROUP

Subsidiary Accounts in Local Currencies, 1973–4

	U.K. Accounts £'000		Australian Accounts $Aus '000		New Zealand Accounts $NZ '000		U.S.A. Accounts $US '000		Canadian Accounts $Can '000	
	1974	1973	1974	1973	1974	1973	1974	1973	1974	1973
Sales	183631	105840	169517	151248	139438	124490	127874	95463	99663	79923
Expenses	179525	102836	160040	141472	130317	115364	126235	94823	93216	75718
Profit before tax	4106	3014	9477	9776	9121	9126	1639	640	6447	4205
Assets Employed	47809	39635	103865	101647	56527	53208	5534	3455	20727	11378
Sales Increment	73.5%		12.08%		12.0%		33.9%		24.7%	
PBT Increment	36.2%		− 3.06%		− 0.05%		156.1%		53.3%	
PBT / Assets Ratio	8.6%	7.6%	9.6%	9.1%	16.1%	17.15%	29.6%	18.5%	31.1%	36.9%

Notes: (1) The Australian company obtained 36% of pretax profit and used 34% of its assets in non-agricultural business.

(2) The New Zealand company obtained 75% of volume and profit from agriculture.

EXHIBIT 2   The Dalgety Group

Balance Sheets as at 30 June 1974

Parent Company				Group	
1973 £000's	*1974* £000's		*Notes*	*1974* £000's	*1973* £000's
22,692	23,171	Issued Ordinary Shares	7	23,171	22,692
15,819	16,565	Share Premium	9	16,565	15,819
19,854	19,848	Reserves	9	54,789	37,570
58,365	59,584	Ordinary Shareholders' Funds		94,525	76,081
3,300	4,633	Preference Shares	7	4,633	3,300
—	—	Minority Shareholder's Interest		7,930	8,121
20,598	21,512	Loan Capital	8	49,658	38,123
—	25	Deferred Taxation	10	3,533	3,439
82,263	85,754	Capital Employed		160,279	129,064
756	6,254	Cash, Bank Balances and Deposits	11	15,365	9,525
1,343	2,991	Debtors		64,578	53,470
—	—	Pastoral Advances		41,262	26,068
—	—	Stocks	12	66,057	41,918
2,099	9,245	Current Assets		187,262	130,981
—	16	Short Term Borrowings	13	67,032	32,080
1,130	1,256	Creditors and Clients' Balances		51,961	42,623
1,745	2,778	Taxation		9,521	6,316
1,796	1,849	Dividents Proposed and Declared		1,849	1,796
734	298	Provisions	14	3,110	3,397
5,585	6,197	Deduct Current Liabilities		133,473	86,212
(3,486)	3,048	Net Current Assets/(Liabilities)		53,789	44,769
85,372	82,432	Subsidiary Companies	15	—	544
193	186	Investments	16	2,623	3,107
—	—	Associated Companies	17	9,318	4,058
184	88	Fixed Assets	18	70,522	57,715
—	—	Goodwill on Consolidation	19	24,027	18,871
82,263	85,754	Net Assets		160,279	129,064

R A Withers, *Chairman and Managing Director*
M J Dowdy, *Director*

EXHIBIT 3 The Dalgety Group

Group Profit and Loss Account for the Year ended 30th June 1974

	Notes	1974 £000's	1974 £000's	1973 £000's	1973 £000's
Group Profit before taxation:	2				
Dalgety Limited and subsidiary companies			19,180		14,946
Associated Companies			(28)		316
			19,152		15,262
Taxation:					
Dalgety Limited and subsidiary companies	4	8,904		6,994	
Associated Companies		79	8,983	156	7,150
Group Profit for the year after taxation			10,169		8,112
Minority Shareholders' proportion of profits less losses of partly-owned subsidiaries			1,173		1,176
Group Profit after taxation attributable to members of Dalgety Limited before extraordinary items			8,996		6,936
Extraordinary Items less provisions for taxation and minority interests where appropriate	3		727		878
Profits Available for Appropriation			9,723		7,814
Dividends	5		1,782		1,834
Profits for the year Retained:	9				
Dalgety Limited		18		2,431	
Subsidiary Companies		8,013		3,484	
Associated Companies		(90)	7,941	65	5,980
Earnings Per Share	6				
Basic			38.4p		29.9p
Fully Diluted			36.3p		28.0p

EXHIBIT 4   The Dalgety Group

Sources and Application of Funds	Actual changes during year (Note a) £'000's	Changes arising from Foreign Exchange Variations £'000's	Changes arising from Acquisition/ Disposal of Subsidiaries £'000's	Total Move-ments on Accounts (Note b) £'000's
Operation:				
Profit after taxation	8,996	—	—	8,996
Extraordinary items	727	—	—	727
Unreleased gain on foreign exchange	—	9,553	—	9,553
Adjustment for items not involving movement of funds:				
Minority interest in profits and extraordinary items	1,507	927	—	2,434
Change in deferred tax	(70)	162	2	94
Depreciation	4,442	—	—	4,442
Other items	—	—	904	904
	15,602	10,642	906	27,150
Less: Dividends paid by company and subsidiaries	(2,135)	—	—	(2,135)
	13,467	10,642	906	25,015
Increase in Loan Capital	14,395	2,112	(817)	15,690
Issue of share capital by company and subsidiaries	3,416	—	—	3,416
Disposal of fixed assets	2,278	—	—	2,278
Sales of subsidiaries	1,196	—	(1,196)	—
Sales of investments	883	(399)	—	484
Sources of Funds	35,635	12,355	(1,107)	46,883
Purchase of fixed assets	12,538	5,945	1,044	19,527
Increase in investments in Associated companies	4,710	535	15	5,260
Increase in current portion of loan cpital	4,155	—	—	4,155
Acquisition of minority interests	1,000	—	2,490	3,490
Increase in Goodwill	333	628	4,195	5,156
Purchase of subsidiaries	7,008	—	(7,008)	—
Other items	—	—	275	275
Application of Funds	29,744	7,108	1,011	37,863
Increase in Net Current Assets	5,891	5,247	(2,118)	9,020
Decrease/(Increase) in Short Term Borrowings	(31,034)	(3,081)	(837)	(34,952)
Increase/(Decrease) in other Working Capital	36,925	8,328	(1,281)	43,972
Increase in Net Current Assests	5,891	5,247	(2,118)	9,020

Notes   (a)   Actual changes during year are those sources and application of funds generated after excluding foreign exchange variations, and acquisitions and disposals of subsidiaries.

(b)   Movements on Accounts represent changes as reflected by the balance sheet and profit and loss account.

EXHIBIT 5 The Dalgety Group

Translation of 1974 Accounts, June 1974 Rates

Sales	Australia	$	169517	at	1.61	=	£	105948
	New Zealand	$	139438	at	1.65			84508
	U.S.A.	$	127874	at	2.40			53281
	Canada	$	99663	at	2.32			42958
	U.K.	£	183631	at	1.00			183631
							£	470326
Expenses	Australia	$	160040	at	1.61	=	£	100025
	New Zealand	$	130317	at	1.65			78980
	U.S.A.	$	126235	at	2.40			52597
	Canada	$	93216	at	2.32			40179
	U.K.	£	179525	at	1.00			179525
							£	(451307)
Central expenses								(133)
Group profit before tax							£	19152

Note: this method was chosen by the company.

EXHIBIT 6 The Dalgety Group

Translation of 1974 Accounts, Temporal Method Approximated

Sales	Australia	$	169517	at	1.61	=	£	105948
	New Zealand	$	139438	at	1.65			84508
	U.S.A.	$	127874	at	2.40			53281
	Canada	$	99663	at	2.32			42958
	U.K.	£	183631	at	1.00			183621
							£	470326
Expenses	Australia	$	160040	at	1.84	=	£	86978
	New Zealand	$	130317	at	1.87			69730
	U.S.A.	$	126235	at	2.58			48928
	Canada	$	93216	at	2.55			36555
	U.K.	£	179525	at	1.00			179525
							£	(421716)
Central expenses								(133)
							£	48477

Note: the above calculation is an approximation to the results which would be obtained with the temporal method of currency translation on the basis of assumptions as to the ages of the assets in each country, which assumptions have not been endorsed or denied by the company.

Note: the exchange rates applied to the sales figures are the average rates for the year end June 1974. By coincidence these rates are the same as the closing rates.

EXHIBIT 7   The Dalgety Group

Some Indices of Price from the IMF International Financial Statistics

Country	Index	4/72	1/73	2/73	3/73	4/73	1/74	2/74	3/74	4/74	
					End of Quarter Value						
Australia	Exchange Rate	1.275	1.417	1.417	1.49	1.488	1.488	1.488	1.31	1.327	U.S. $ per Aust. $
	Wool Export Price	218	311	250	276	252	222	173	148	168	Index of price, 1970 = 100
	Wheat Export Price	157	155	156	250	278	303	264	245	314	Index of price, 1970 = 100
	Beef Export Price	121	127	145	147	160	145	120	101	97	Index of price, 1970 = 100
	Consumer Price	114	117	120	125	129	132	138	145	151	Consumer Price Index
New Zealand	Exchange Rate	1.1962	1.327	1.327	1.48	1.43	1.47	1.45	1.3	1.32	U.S. $ per N.Z. $
	Wool Export Price	194	247	271	272	272	168	150	143	142	Index, 1970 = 100
	Lamb Export Price	128	134	147	156	175	117	124	128	123	Index, 1970 = 100
	CPI	120	123	126	129	132	136	139	144	149	Consumer Price Index
U.S.A.	Exchange Rate	1.08	1.21	1.21	1.21	1.21	1.21	1.21	1.19	1.22	U.S. $ per IMF Special Drawing Right
	Consumer Price	109	111	113	116	118	122	125	129	133	CPI, 1970 = 100
	Import Prices	117	121	131	136	147	172	196	210	217	Import Price Index, 1970 = 100
Canada	Exchange Rate	.99	.99	.99	1.0	.99	.97	.97	.98	.99	Canadian $ per U.S. $
	Wood Pulp Export	94	98	106	119	134	149	171	195	211	Export Price Index, 1970 = 100
	Consumer Price	100	112	114	118	120	123	127	131	134	CPI, 1970 = 100
U.K.	Exchange Rate	2.35	2.48	2.58	2.41	2.32	2.39	2.39	2.33	2.34	U.S. $ per £ Sterling
	CPI	121	123	127	129	133	139	147	151	158	Index, 1970 = 100

EXHIBIT 8   The Dalgety Group

Currently Translated, Local General Price Level Adjusted Accounts, 1974

	Australia				Deflated in U.K.	New Zealand*	U.S.A.*	Canada*	U.K.*	Consolidation
	Local Currency	Local Price Level Factor	Deflated Local	Translation Factor						
Sales	169517	138/131	178575	1.61	110916	87661	55733	43174	197035	493519
Expenses	160040	138/123	179557	1.61	(111526)	(86442)	(57915)	(41486)	(206173)	503542
Inflation Adjustment			16782	1.61	10426	6448	2936	2202	14660	36670
Contribution to Group					9814	7667	756	2890	5522	26647
New Net Assets	12465	138/131	13131	1.61	8156	5365	1251	4370	16710	35852
Older Net Assets	100877	138/114	122114	1.61	75857	40095	2065	7907	44150	170064
Equity	103865	138/120	119445	1.61	74189	37793	2562	9387	55338	179269

* These were derived in the same fashion as Australia

EXHIBIT 9 The Dalgety Group

Temporally Translated, General Price Level Adjusted Accounts, 1974

	Australia			UK Consumer Price Factor	UK Inflation Adjusted	New Zealand	U.S.A.*	Canada*	U.K.*	Consolidation
	Local Currency	Translation Factor	Translated							
Sales	169517	1.6	105948	147/137	113681	90676	57170	46094	197035	504656
Expenses	160040	1.84	86978	147/128	(99889)	(80032)	(56191)	(41981)	(206173)	(484266)
Currency Adjustment			14555	147/147	(14555)	(9064)	(3544)	(3464)	—	(30627)
Inflation					8295	6376	3502	2797	14661	35631
Contribution to Group					7532	7956	937	3446	5523	25394
New Net Assets	12465	1.6	7791	147/137	8360	5355	1277	4467	16711	36170
Older Net Assets	100877	1.88	53658	147/121	65188	36328	2143	8387	44150	156196
Equity	103865	1.82	57034	147/127	66016	33727	2483	9408	55338	166972

* These were derived in the same fashion as Australia.

EXHIBIT 10   The Dalgety Group

Currently Translated, Local Special Price Level Adjusted Accounts, 1974

	Australia					New Zealand*	U.S.A.*	Canada*	U.K.*	Consolidated Accounts
	Local Accounts	Local Special Price Level Factor	Deflated Local	Current Exchange	U.K. Accounts					
Sales	169517	173/231	126954	1.61	78853	58959	64336	48446	197035	447629
Expenses	160040	173/272	(101790)	1.61	(63224)	(44538)	(77256)	(56839)	(206173)	(448030)
Inflation			(7636)	1.61	(4743)	(3012)	13916	12279	14661	33101
Contribution to Group					10886	11409	996	3886	5523	32700
New Net Assets	12465	173/231	9335	1.61	5798	3608	1444	5020	16711	32581
Older Net Assets	100877	173/218	80054	1.61	49723	26764	3017	12459	44150	136113
Equity	103865	173/250	71861	1.61	44634	18962	3464	13592	55338	135990

* These were derived in the same fashion as Australia.

EXHIBIT 11 The Dalgety Group

Summary of Results after Inflation and Exchanges Adjustments

Translation Method		Current	Current	Temporal
Inflation Adjustment Method		Local General Price Level	Local Special Price Level	U.K. General Price Level
Source Exhibit		H	J	I
Australia	Sales	110916	78853	113681
	Expenses	111526	63226	99889
	Profit	−610	15629	13792
	Assets	84003	55521	73548
	PBT/Assets	Loss	28%	18.8%
New Zealand	Sales	87661	55521	73548
	Expenses	86442	44538	80032
	Profit	1219	14421	10644
	Assets	45460	30372	41683
	PBT/Assets	2.7%	47%	25.5%
U.S.A.	Sales	55733	64336	57170
	Expenses	57915	77256	56191
	Profit	−2182	−12920	979
	Assets	3316	4461	3420
	PBT/Assets	Loss	Loss	28.6%
Canada	Sales	42174	48446	46094
	Expenses	41486	56839	41981
	Profit	688	−8393	4113
	Assets	12277	17479	12854
	PBT / Assets	5.6%	Loss	32%
U.K.	Sales	197035	197035	197035
	Expenses	206173	206173	206173
	Profit	−9138	−9138	−9138
	Assets	60861	60861	60861
	PBT/Assets	Loss	Loss	Loss

7 Elliott Products Ltd

Mr James Hunt joined the Anderson Paper and Packaging Group in March 1968 as a member of the main board and chairman of two of the company's operating subsidiaries. Prior to joining Anderson he had been 30 years with one of the largest companies in the paper industry, primarily in the financial function but also with experience in general management, including a period as managing director of a case-making subsidiary. A few days after his appointment with Anderson he received a memorandum from Mr Eric Syme, managing director of Elliott Products Limited, one of the two subsidiaries for which he was responsible, asking him to sponsor before the main board a capital expenditure proposal. The proposal entailed an investment of about £170,000 in facilities to produce disposable plastic cups, and showed an expected return in excess of 40 per cent (see Exhibit 6).

Investment projects above £20,000 required authorisation by the main board before they could be undertaken. After considering the plastic cup proposal with some care Mr Hunt had decided to request the board at its June meeting to approve its immediate implementation.

ANDERSON PAPER AND PACKAGING GROUP

The Anderson Paper and Packaging Group was formed by a merger early in 1966 between Anderson Paper Company (APC) and Stewarts (packaging) Limited (SPL). For APC this was the culmination of ten years of takeover activity which transformed the company from being predominantly a wrapping paper manufacturer to an integrated paper group, with activities extending right through to the ultimate customer.

Under increasing competitive pressure, APC established in 1956 its own selling and distribution organisation – a new area for a management which had been traditionally production-oriented – thereby eliminating its previous dependence on the merchanting trade. After this had been successfully achieved APC embarked upon a policy of growth by acquisition, directed towards achieving a broader spectrum of activities primarily in the converted paper products area. In the five years between 1958 and 1963 APC made a number of acquisitions, including Mitchells Ltd, a sizeable vertically integrated paper and packaging group, and early in 1963 Elliott Products Limited. During the following three years takeover activity was suspended as the considerable task of absorption, reorganisation and rationalisation of the greatly expanded group was undertaken.

Early in 1966, the Calvert Company, a similar-sized paper group, unexpectedly announced a bid for APC. Rejecting this, APC through its financial advisers revealed that merger negotiations were in train with SPL, a company involved in bag-making, printing, flexible packaging and carton manufacture. Negotiations were hastened to a conclusion, with an agreed price of £8.1 million giving the former APC shareholders and management control of the new organisation, Anderson Paper and Packaging Group.

The ensuing examination and analysis of SPL's operations and accounts suggested that Anderson's management had before it at least another two years of rationalisation activity. Within less than twelve months Anderson was the subject of another bid, this time from a major U.S. paper group, which planned to amalgamate Anderson with its

---

The names of the companies involved, the industry, and the figures in the case have all been disguised.

already extensive facilities in Britain. Worth £35 million, the bid valued Anderson's shares at 85p compared with a pre-bid market price of 45½p. On the grounds of the monopolistic implications, Anderson's management succeeded in having the bid referred to the Board of Trade, which subsequently requested its withdrawal.

Exhibit 1 presents selected financial information on Anderson Paper between 1957 and 1967.

The objectives of the much-enlarged group had been described by the chairman at a press conference after the SPL acquisition as follows:

Anderson Paper and Packaging Group, as its name suggests, manufactures and sells converted paper products. The means to achieving this purpose are our paper and board mills and converting plants.

Our objective is to determine which are the paper products where growth prospects exist and where we have the appropriate skills. Our pool of these has expanded considerably in the last decade, as you will realise.

After identifying the growth areas – a continuing task in this rapidly developing world – we shall aim at winning and then maintaining significant market shares. By redeploying our capital in this way we shall eliminate the unevenness in return on capital which currently exists across the group.'

ELLIOTT PRODUCTS LIMITED

The purchase of Elliott Products was part of the growth and development plan of the Anderson paper Company. In 1963 the chairman of APC described the acquisition as follows:

Elliott manufactures and markets a comprehensive range of high-quality paper bags, disposable paper drinking cups and allied products. For many years they have been purchasing a sizeable proportion of their raw material requirements from us. The Elliott management has in recent years been extending activities with ventures in polythene laminates and other flexible packagings to compensate for any possible decline in their present paper products. These activities fit in well with Anderson's and the acquisition will prove a source of strength to us.

Elliott Paper Bag Company was founded towards the end of the nineteenth century at Otley on the outskirts of London. In the period up to 1939 the company became a leading supplier in the U.K. of paper bags and disposable paper cups.

After the war expansion continued: six acquisitions were made in as many years, three in related fields and the others, in three different areas. The former three comprised: a small paper mill supplying part of Elliott's requirements; Hadley Brothers Ltd, a manufacturer and distributor of and an outlet for Elliott's disposable paper cups; and a half-share in a smaller bag producer. Market prospects constrained further expansion in the traditional product fields although the returns from both – particularly disposable paper cups – remained good. By the middle of the 1950s trading profits approached £1 million a year. Further diversification had been judged to be undesirable and by 1958 liquid reserves, invested in government securities, totalled almost £2 million.

In 1958 Elliott was taken over by a smaller diversified group operating in unrelated markets. Over the following four years Elliott's traditional product lines were expanded to take account of market developments: for example, the threat to paper cups arising from plastic containers was met by developing the manufacturing capability to make plastic cups in Hadley Brothers, and distributing these under Hadley and Elliott brand names. In addition, a small company making paper and polythene laminates was put under Elliott's management.[1]

In 1963 Anderson Paper Company, anxious to secure the paper sales of a problematic mill in Scotland, of which Elliott was a major customer, purchased for £1.1 million the traditional activities of Elliott, together with the laminating plant.[2] The combined performance of these units between 1958 and 1962 is shown in Exhibit 2. Together with the Scottish mill and another APC paper mill, these facilities were grouped under Elliott management into a new division entitled Industrial Packaging.[3] Over the next three years the division underwent many changes: an industrial paper products converter was purchased to provide a captive outlet for spare capacity of the ex-APC mill; a half-share in the Scottish mill was sold and control relinquished; the small bag factory, of which Elliott had previously acquired a half-share, was closed; and subsequently the ex-APC mill was shut down.

Concurrently a new product policy for the company within the APC framework was being developed by the divisional chairman, Mr Ainsworth, previously managing director of Elliott from 1958. Based on the laminating capability, it envisaged Elliott as the vehicle for entry into the growing field of flexible packagings. However, these plans lapsed. Serious problems elsewhere in the group occupied Mr Ainsworth, by now a group board member and chairman of a second division, and the SPL merger in 1966 continued this situation. Moreover, it became known in 1964 that the Otley site, where it had been planned to concentrate all production, including polythene laminating, lay in the path of a proposed ring road development. It was not until late 1967, after some three years of uncertainty, that the final line was fixed, which revealed that one-tenth of the site would be lost. Negotiations over compensation were not completed until 1968, after Mr Hunt's arrival, when it was indicated that the land would be required, cleared, by January 1971.

The managing director of Elliott throughout this period (since 1963) was Mr Eric Syme. He had joined the company in 1955 as sales manager and had then served for several years as deputy to Mr Ainsworth. His marketing training convinced him of the importance of staying closely attuned to his customers' needs, a belief which contributed to his individual view as to the future direction of Elliott:

Elliott is not a paper company, it just happens traditionally to have used paper base materials. Nor does it have any outstanding expertise in coating and laminating in a technical sense. Elliott's strengths are in its distribution channels where it has a strong brand name, a reputation for good quality and almost one hundred years of experience in serving the bag wholesaling and catering materials suppliers trades.

These strengths he had for some time wished to exploit more fully, particularly by having Elliott invest in its own sheet and thermo-forming plant for plastic cups.

GROUP ORGANISATION AND REPORTING PROCEDURES

Anderson Paper and Packaging Group had a decentralised structure, with the group board directors as chairmen of operating divisions and subsidiaries performing a liaison and interpretive role. This organisation, in the words of the 'Procedure

---

[1] Paper and polythene laminates consisted of thin sheets of paper and polythene bonded together to form a strong, light and flexible material. It overcame many of the problems which paper had faced as a packaging material, making it directly competitive with more traditional packaging materials such as jute bags.

[2] That is to say, APC acquired Elliott's paper bag and cup manufacturing activities along with the laminating plant. Hadley Brothers was not acquired.

[3] Although called the Industrial Packaging Division, the legal entity 'Elliott Products Limited' continued in existence. In the group's reporting system and in management's conversation it was common to refer to the trading unit as 'Elliott', not as the Industrial Packaging Division.

Manual' issued to senior group management and those responsible for the management of operating units, was 'designed to grant substantial independence to . . . subsidiary management to enable profits to be maximised within the framework of overall group objectives and strategies'. The procedures it laid down were considered to represent the 'minimum interferences . . . from the centre compatible with adequate financial planning, control and communication'. They covered four broad areas:[4]

(1) Standard forms of accounts and schedules, for accounts consolidation.

(2) Profit planning (including budgeting).

(3) Submission of control information to group headquarters.

(4) Capital expenditure proposals, along with an overall capital budget.

The annual profit plan and reporting of results constituted the 'instrument of coordination, planning and control'. This approach, the Procedures Manual explained, was based on:

(1) Defining the objectives of the division / subsidiary.

(2) Estimating the impact on profits of attaining these objectives.

(3) Analysing the subsequent operating performance to indicate successes, failures or changes of direction.

Both objectives and management performance were assessed by various criteria: e.g. survival and innovation; growth; market share; cash flow; absolute profit size; and return on capital employed. However, particular emphasis was accorded return on capital and the comparison of actual and planned performance.

Planned and actual performance of Elliott Products since 1964 is shown in Exhibit 3.

When Mr Hunt joined Anderson, Elliott's profit plan and budget for 1968 was awaiting appraisal. Included in it was a proposal for investing in the necessary machinery for the manufacture of plastic cups by the vacuum forming process.

THE PLASTIC CUP PROJECT

Events Leading up to the Situation in 1968

About the time of Mr Syme's joining Elliott in 1955, a number of U.S. companies were conducting experiments with high-impact polystyrene cups as substitutes for the traditional paper cup. In the light of the favourable results reported in the States, sheet making and forming machinery was installed by Elliott at the Otley plant, but was not put into production due to opposition from the chairman. Realising its potential, the Hadley representative on Elliott's board succeeded in having the machinery transferred to its North East factory just before the takeover of Elliott in 1958.

From remarks made by his sales team Mr Syme began to discern an emerging demand for plastic cups. However, at that time the group company, Hadley Brothers Ltd, was still in the process of developing its own plastic cup range as part of a reorganisation programme. When it became available in 1962 it was marketed both by Hadley under the name 'Moderna' through its own distributors and other dealers, and by Elliott under its disposable paper cup brand name 'Regal'.

---

[4] In addition there were regulations on matters such as insurance and notes on recommended techniques, e.g. DCF in capital budgeting.

This supply arrangement with Hadley continued after the transfer of ownership of Elliott to APC in 1963, but over the next year or so the relationship with Hadley became strained as a result of fluctuating product quality. Thus, in 1964 notice of termination of the contract at the year-end was given.

Among the alternatives then examined was installing sheet and thermo-forming plant at Otley, but the idea was rejected. Mr Syme enumerated various considerations which had led to this conclusion, amongst them: surplus capacity at that time in the market was causing margins to be eroded because of high trade and consumer discounts by the manufacturers; Elliott did not feel they could support a direct sales force; the timing was wrong; and the the discounts offered by Cairn, as an alternative supplier to Hadley, were particularly attractive. Also, management effort had to be devoted to increased paper responsibilities, and the laminating plant was being integrated into operations and considerable new capital was to be invested in laminating machinery.

Therefore, in January 1965 a three-year supply contract was signed with Cairn Limited, the market leader and a manufacturer-distributor of plastic cups and other disposable catering products. Elliott's management considered the terms very favourable, with their purchase price being 45 per cent off list. In 1967 gross profit on bought-in plastic cups exceeded 40 per cent. In addition, there was a non-contractual reciprocal product flow, Cairn purchasing a sizeable volume of decorated paper cups, plates and the like for sale through its dealership.

Marketing

The trend in sales of Elliott's disposable paper and plastic products from 1963 to 1967 is presented in Exhibit 4.

Mr Foster, sales director, did not know the overall size of the market, but he was aware that for many years before he joined the company in 1965 Elliott had been the predominant producer of paper-based disposable products with its 'Regal' brand. Obversely, it was equally clear to him that Elliott's market position in plastic-based products was much less significant and its reputation on quality and delivery unreliable.

Among the leading firms in the U.K. disposable catering products market Elliott alone did not possess its own distribution outlets. This had not always been the case: in the 1950s, when Hadley Brothers Ltd was part of the Elliott group it provided captive outlets, although these had by no means been used exclusively. At that time, neither Hadley nor the other catering materials suppliers had any great capacity to manufacture their own disposable products ranges but just as Hadley moved into plastic cup production in the early 1960s so too did its principal rivals.

In 1967 the largest of these manufacturer-distributors was Cairn, which in the previous two years had absorbed both Hadley, at that time a fierce price-cutter, and another similar concern. The other leading firm, also a manufacturer-distributor, was Polycups Limited which had recently been taken over by a diversified American company.

In all there were some 200 distributors, of which Mr Foster considered about 40 to be important.

Mr Foster explained the competitive situation: 'The largest manufacturer/ distributor organisations all make their own plastic cups and the like, sell both direct and through distributors and have local representation.[5] In addition they have, until recently, been engaged in a vicious price war offering large discounts both direct and to distributors'.

---

[5] The distributors were wholesalers, selling to retail outlets and directly to major users, such as operators of vending machines. There were literally thousands of outlets for plastic cups, and other disposable catering products, throughout the country, but only about two hundred of these accounted individually for a significant volume of purchases and sales.

'Regal' paper and plastic products were sold through all the important distributors, including those of Cairn and Polycups. One representative was fully employed selling disposable catering products: with the large distributors he dealt with the central offices, and he called on the smaller distributors individually.

Sheet and Thermo-forming Equipment Investment

In 1966, not long after the problems stemming from the merger with SPL had begun to dominate group attention, Eric Syme – by that time managing director of Elliott's – made a visit to the U.S.A. to attend the U.S. Packaging Fair, a bi-annual event which he had been attending since he joined Elliott Products.

During discussions with the vice-president of Melville Craig Co., a disposable plastic products manufacturer with which he had established contact during the 1962 Fair, he determined that the firm would be willing to provide engineering specifications and production know-how on the vacuum forming plant[6] it had developed and was operating. For cost and import duty reasons, Mr Syme envisaged construction of the plant in the U.K. Subsequently terms were agreed comprising $27,000 for plant specifications (and any subsequent improvements) and a royalty of 2 per cent on net sales for a period of 5 years.

On his return from the U.S.A. Mr Syme prepared for his directors a memorandum which appraised the whole subject of Elliott undertaking its own vacuum forming. On the question of alternative sources of the necessary technical expertise, he stated:

First you must consider whether the information Melville Craig is willing to provide could be obtained elsewhere more cheaply. Such possible sources appear to be:

(a) petrochemical firms which produce the plastic base material. Possibly free?

(b) an expert in these techniques, in which case the cost would be his salary plus maintenance;

(c) another company as qualified as Melville Craig, but at a lower price;

(d) a published literature search.

As regards (a) and (b) there would undoubtedly be a period of trial before we became operational, which must be considered as an extra cost. Alternative (d) I am sure you will agree involves too much time, effort and cost with no guarantee of success.

It is my opinion that an agreement with Melville Craig, with whom we have an excellent relationship, could not be bettered.

Impressed by the possibilities of the proposal and encouraged by the market potential in the rapidly expanding automatic vending field, the Elliott board approved a technical and cost evaluation agreement with Melville Craig. This appraisal, which was carried out in August 1967 by the production director, Mr Young, and his chief engineer, was favourable on both counts. For the product specification required for the U.K. market plant output on three shifts would be of the order of 60 million units a year. Besides approving of the equipment for plastic vending cup manufacture they drew attention to the fact that it could with only minor modification produce a range of containers for the convenience food industry, an activity which was described as 'profitable in the extreme to Melville Craig'. As regards financial projections, Mr Young made a profitability study which he compared with a similar calculation

---

[6] There are two production stages in manufacturing plastic containers: first plastic sheet is made from granules, then it is made into the container by a thermal forming process. In the case of plastic vending cups this process is vacuum forming.

assuming continuation of the Cairn agreement. Thermo-forming by Elliott appeared to be the more attractive proposition.

Preparation of the Investment Plan

In the light of this favourable report, Mr Syme instructed his sales director to prepare a marketing strategy and sales forecast for Elliott-produced polystyrene drinking cups.

Mr Foster, taking as his starting point the position that Elliott had only a 'rudimentary selling organisation and little sales', considered the company's objectives should be to retain as much paper cup sales as possible while achieving a 10 per cent penetration of the plastic cup market within three years. Estimating U.K. capacity for thermo-forming of high-impact polystyrene cups[7] at about 1,000 million units per year, he argued:

> Ten per cent of this total of 100 million units. Compared with present sales of about 30 million units this means we must boost sales by 70 million units in three years. To achieve this we must turn to the possibility of direct sales. There we would enjoy bigger margins even if we had to engage in price competition (which would not be our intention) and the only possible loss would be the distributor business which is not a sizeable proportion, given that we could still retain our major customer.[8]
> I thus propose a sales team comprising a new sales manager and five direct salesmen, each with a target of 20 million cups p.a. within three years. On this basis, we shall achieve the required extra sales during the second year of operation.
> Besides the polystyrene cups, the team will be expected to promote sales of our waxed paper cups.

The sales forecasts made by Mr Foster, given the alternatives of continuing buying-in or self-manufacture, provided the basis for net sales in Exhibit 5. Given these, Mr Syme had prepared factory profitability projections, which assumed in the case of self-manufacture beginning operations on one unit at the start of 1969 and phasing in another in the second half of 1970. The projections, based on the assumption of the continuation of constant 1967 material costs, expenses and selling values, are presented in Exhibit 5. The annual royalty charge of 2 per cent on net sales payable for five years was deducted in arriving at net sales under self-manufacture and the initial know-how fee of $27,000 was included in factory overheads.

Capital expenditure before grants was estimated at £80,500 in 1968 and a further £76,400 in 1969/70 for the second unit. Mr Syme went on:

> A suitable production area is immediately available and the reconstruction interference does not arise. Suitable qualified staff would also be immediately available. Melville Craig have promised continuing consultation on the operation of the equipment plus additional engineering changes and updating as it may develop. They would also make available people to assist in erecting our plant.

Mr Syme had not found it easy to determine return on capital:

> It is difficult to calculate accurately net profitability of plastic cups, or any other product. I have considered overhead allocation on both volume and activity bases to arrive at the stated results. The projected increases largely concern additional selling expenses, including commission.

---

[7] Plastic cups made from moulded expanded polystyrene were also made, but represented an insignificant part of the total market.
[8] At that time this customer accounted for one-fifth of total sales.

The outcome of his calculations, set out in Exhibit 6, was an expected return on capital of 43 per cent in 1970 and 46 per cent in 1973. 'Even under very depressed terms – i.e. after inflating projected discounts by another 15–20 per cent', Mr Syme calculated, 'the return is still approximately 25 per cent'.

Mr Syme was encouraged by the results of this detailed examination of the project's viability; the more so because by the latter part of 1967 he was becoming increasingly anxious about the security of the revenue from the bought-in plastic cups. On the one hand it had become a significant element in overall gross profit, approaching £40,000 per year at a time when revenue from their paper products was declining and other product lines were being rationalised; on the other, dealings with Cairn had not been entirely satisfactory.

In the document supporting the vacuum forming machinery investment, which accompanied Elliott's 1968 Profit Plan, Mr Syme had catalogued a number of adverse experiences with Cairn over the previous twelve months. Primary amongst these were that Cairn had made it known to some customers that they manufactured on behalf of Elliott; they had altered product specification without prior notification or approval; and they had caused lost business through late delivery. Regular pressure was now required to receive supplies within eight weeks.

Mr Syme concluded his analysis as follows:

Plastic cups have already successfully recovered some of the declining paper cup revenue. No alternative equally profitable product line has been identified for immediate exploitation. It is the Elliott view that this revenue should be safeguarded and extended. It is held that to achieve this now requires prompt action to make Elliott self-sufficient in plastic cup manufacture.

MR HUNT'S ASSESSMENT OF THE PROPOSAL

Mr Hunt joined Anderson Paper at an opportune time in the sense that the profit plans for the financial year beginning 1 April 1968 were on the point of being submitted to head office by the operating units. Within a few days of taking up the chairmanship of Elliott Products he had before him for review and appraisal the subsidiary's 1968/69 Profit Plan and a document entitled 'Sheet and Thermo-forming Equipment Investment', submitted in accordance with procedure to support the investment proposal in the plan.

Mr Hunt had not received a brief concerning either Anderson or Elliott. As regards Anderson, he was of course aware in general terms from working elsewhere in the industry of its recent activities and the problems it faced. Indeed, the tasks required of senior management were such that he saw the role of a group board director as chairman of an operating unit as, temporarily, more executive than liaison in nature.

Even though this was not regarded as a satisfactory situation, rather than simply ensuring that unit policy was compatible with overall group strategy, it was felt that in the short term the group executives should be directly involved in important decision-making at the operating level.

Mr Hunt found that he learned a considerable amount about Elliott from a fairly intensive examination of the budgeted sales figures, costs and so on over a two-week period. He explained how he approached appraising the plan:

I was obviously not in any position to say increase it by five or reduce it by ten, but solely to try to establish its credibility, which I did in some detail with the sort of approach a consultant would have.

From the profit plan and conversations about it with the Elliott executives, Mr Hunt formed an impression of Elliott as a company involved in bag making and the production of disposable cups, plates, and other containers for the catering market. The polythene laminating activities seemed to be of less importance.

On studying the capital expenditure document and discussing it with Mr Syme, Mr Hunt formed three initial impressions about the proposal to purchase the vacuum forming plant for plastic cup manufacture. Firstly, it was apparent that Elliott had a successful, profitable and growing business selling bought-in plastic cups. However, competing against the largest supplier in the market with its own product obviously entailed a commercial risk. Further, it seemed that the production technology involved in the project was outside Elliott's normal technology.

As he looked further into the project, Mr Hunt learned that there was a considerable background of thinking and analysis on the matter. Old papers sent to the previous chairman showed that it had been canvassed over a period of years, a fact which was confirmed by Mr Syme and Mr Ainsworth (managing director of Elliott from 1958 to 1963).

He did not undertake any special research himself:

> I think as a new chairman you have to take things on trust to some extent. If you were to come in and say that you were not going to make any decisions until you understood the business thoroughly, then everything would grind to a halt.

In view of the anxiety expressed by Mr Syme about the insecurity of the current supply relationship, Mr Hunt insisted at an early stage on visiting Cairn's managing director, which Mr Syme was easily able to arrange on the grounds of introducing Elliott's new chairman. The outcome was that Mr Hunt fully endorsed Mr Syme's viewpoint. Indeed, he felt that the competitive market positions of the two companies rendered the relationship inevitably insecure:

> The judgment I came to was that the arrangement was fraught with the risk all the time of being cut off for any of a number of reasons.

On marketing and profitability grounds, Mr Hunt considered there were no serious grounds for concern. Elliott, he felt, possessed a valuable market position as established and respected suppliers of high-quality disposable paper cups and allied products, which would carry over into marketing plastic products of a similar nature. Commercial success of the project he considered likely on the following grounds:

> Elliott has been for a long time a leading supplier of paper cups and the like and has sustained sales of these products at surprisingly high levels in view of the performance and price disadvantages which they suffer. This argues a skill in marketing and a goodwill in the market place to be able to maintain an expensive, obsolescent material against a modern one.

Mr Hunt had a certain concern about the planned marketing strategy of a small direct selling team competing against the extensive field forces of the large manufacturer-distributors. However, for two reasons he did not consider this to be a major problem. On the one hand, it was his experience that a trade did not like to be in the hands of just a few large suppliers. He would call to mind several instances of smaller, respected companies obtaining a significant market share on this basis. Secondly, he did not believe a sizeable new marketing load would be created, since the product would go through traditional outlets, being handled by traditional product salesmen. He saw self-manufactured plastic cups merely as a replacement for the bought-in product which in turn was merely a replacement for paper cups.

Mr Hunt summarised his feeling on marketing in the following terms:

> If it were a product for an entirely new market, then I would not support the

proposal. The only reason for doing so is to ride on the back, so to speak, of an established marketing position.

The forecast profitability was very substantial. It was Mr Hunt's opinion that even if a DCF analysis were used, the investment would pay for itself easily on a cash flow basis. An analysis of this type had not been used by Elliott, but Mr Hunt did not consider it necessary at this juncture: 'If you get a return of 40 per cent or more then the DCF is all right.'

Not long after his meeting with Cairn, Mr Hunt met a senior executive of Melville Craig who was visiting Britain. He was impressed: 'As far as I can determine they have a very high standing both technically and as a reputable company.' This encounter, together with the confidence that the technology could be successfully transferred expressed in the technical evaluation report by Mr Young, whom he regarded as very capable, eased Mr Hunt's misgivings on this issue, although not fully.

One final less tangible matter played a part in Mr Hunt's considerations. He expressed it as follows:

Another point in my mind is that Elliott have been a shrinking company for some time in that its products have been continuously declining. I do not know how much money value you can put on it, but there is an element of wish on my part to allow them to do something positive so as to try to restore some feeling of confidence in themselves and a feeling that the shareholders have confidence in them to launch something new. The amount of money involved is not heavy, so we are not hazarding the company, only a fairly small percentage. I think all these factors come into decisions of this nature.

For these reasons Mr Hunt decided to present the proposal to the main board for approval at its June meeting.

EXHIBIT 1   Anderson Paper Company/Anderson Paper and Packaging Group
(Financial data in £ million)

	[1] 1957/58	1958/59	1959/60	1960/61	1961/62	1962/63	1963/64	1964/65	1965/66	1966/67	1967/68
Turnover	n.a.	n.a.	n.a.	n.a.	17.9	23.0	25.1	25.8	26.7[2]	55.9	54.5
Trading Profit	1.2	1.3	1.4	1.2	1.8	2.5	2.5	2.1	2.7	6.2	5.0
Depreciation	0.4	0.4	0.5	0.5	0.6	0.6	0.8	0.9	1.0	1.6	1.5
Interest	..	..	..	..	0.1	0.3	0.2	0.3	0.4	0.8	0.9
Taxation	0.4	0.4	0.5	0.4	0.5	0.7	0.6	0.4	0.5	1.9	1.3
Net Profit	0.4	0.5	0.4	0.3	0.6	0.9	0.9	0.5	0.8	1.9	1.3
Preference dividends	..	..	..	..	..	..	..	..	..	0.1	0.1
Ordinary dividends	0.2	0.3	0.4	0.3	0.4	0.6	0.8	0.6	0.6	1.3	1.2
Profit retained	0.2	0.2	0.1	0.1	0.3	0.4	0.4	(0.1)	0.1	0.3	(0.1)
Dividend on ordinary shares adjusted for bonus plus rights issues (%)	7.0	7.0	7.0	7.5	8.5	12.0	12.0	10.0	10.0	12.0	12.0
Fixed assets	4.6	4.8	4.9	4.9	6.1	7.1	7.9	8.3	9.4	18.4	17.1
Current assets	6.1	6.5	6.7	6.6	9.9	12.9	13.2	13.5	15.4	25.8	21.6
Current liabilities	2.4	1.9	1.9	1.7	2.2	5.5	4.1	4.9	6.7	12.8	11.3
Long-term debt	1.0	1.0	1.0	1.0	3.1	3.0	2.6	3.6	4.0	9.0	9.4
Ordinary Shareholders investment	6.1	7.1	7.5	7.5	9.5	10.3	13.0	12.5	13.2	19.8	18.6
London prices of 5/- Ordinary shares High	n.a.	n.a.	11/3	8/6	11/10	12/-	13/4	14/6	11/7	10/6	15/3
Low			6/5	6/8	7/3	8/3	9/8	8/2	7/11	7/-	5/3

Notes: n.a. = not available.   .. = less than 0.05
[1] April–March   [2] £50.6 if SPL had been included

Sources: Anderson Paper and Packaging Group: Annual report 1967/68; Financial Press (share prices)

EXHIBIT 2   Elliott Products Limited

Selected Financial Data 1958–1962
(£000)

		1958	1959	1960	1961	1962
Net Assets	(1)	1,128	1,181	1,067	996	1,202
Turnover	(2)	1,857	1,793	1,731	1,639	1,774
Trading Profits	(3)	272	182	181	135	129
Profit % to Net Assets		24.2	15.4	16.9	13.5	10.7
Profit % to Turnover		14.7	10.2	10.4	8.2	7.3

Notes: (1) Trading assets only and excluding cash, bank overdrafts and investments.
(2) Includes intra-company sales.
(3) Excludes exceptional and prior-year items, investment income, interest received or paid and central expenses.

Source: Annual Report of previous owning company

EXHIBIT 3 Elliott Products Limited: Budgeted and Actual Profits 1964–7[1]

Units: £

	1964		1965		1966[1]		1967	
	Budget	Actual	Budget	Actual	Budget	Actual	Budget	Actual
Operating Profits:								
Paper & plastic cups and paper bags[2]	183,591	183,752	186,715	123,612				
All Other[2]	73,101	26,584	44,490	(15,824)[3]				
Total	256,692	210,336	231,205	107,788				
Less: Divisional expenses	134,068	129,277	145,716	143,470				
Divisional Profit before Tax	122,624	81,059	85,489	(35,682)[3]				
Pre-Tax Profits:								
Paper & plastic cups and paper bags[2]					85,121	40,583	46,100	85,875
All Other[2]					27,176	(37,002)[3]	8,500	(7,763)[3]
Total					112,297	3,581	54,600	78,112
Less: Head Office Charge					5,200	3,300	8,300	8,300
Divisional Profit before Tax					107,097	281	46,300	69,812

Notes: 1. Besides the format change, in 1966 the accounting year was changed from March–February to April–March. However, the figures given for 1966 represent 12 months only for reasons of comparison.
2. Also included in the earlier years are paper making activities subsequently transferred or phased out.
3. The figures in brackets are negative.

Source: Company records.

EXHIBIT 4   Elliott Products Limited

Sales of Disposable Catering Products 1963–1967
(Index of sales order 1963 = 100)

	1963	1964	1965	1966	1967
Paper cups	100	102	83	79	76
Other disposable paper products	100	76	76	37	37
Plastic cups	100	106	131	73	95

Source: Company records

EXHIBIT 5 Vacuum Forming Investment: Projected Profitability

	Buying-In				Self-Manufacture			Buying-In		
	1966	*1967 Budget*	*1967 Estimated Actual*	*1968 Budget*	*1969*	*1971*	*1973*	*1969*	*1971*	*1973*
Net Sales¹ (£'000)	64.4	62.8	87.9	108.9	111.5	146.7	219.0	95.1	81.8	67.1
Less: Direct Materials (£'000)	39.7	43.4	48.3	65.0	43.6	58.5	87.4	65.5	56.2	46.2
Other direct² (£'000)	0.6	1.7	2.0	2.5	11.5	17.6	25.6	2.7	2.7	2.7
Gross Profit (£'000)	24.1	17.7	37.6	41.4	56.4	70.6	106.0	26.9	22.9	18.2
–"– (% to Net Sales)	37.4%	28.2%	42.8%	38.0%	50.5%	48.2%	48.4%	28.3%	28.0%	27.1%
Less: Factory Overheads (£'000)	0.5	0.9	0.9	1.2	3.1	3.9	5.4	1.3	1.3	1.3
Factory Profit (£'000)	23.6	16.8	36.9	40.2	53.6	66.7	100.6	25.6	21.6	16.9

Notes: 1. Net of discounts and, in the case of self-manufacture, of royalty payments.
2. Principally direct wages.

Source: Company records.

EXHIBIT 6
A Vacuum-Forming Machinery Investment

Forecast Return on Capital

	£ ooo	
	1970	*1973*
Fixed Assets[1]	49.6	74.3
Stocks[2]	41.3	68.5
Debtors[3]	21.5	36.5
	112.4	179.3
Less: Creditors[4]	6.4	10.9
Net Capital Invested	106.0	168.4

	1966	*1968*	*1970*	*1973*
Factory Profit[5]	23.6	36.9	60.0	100.6
Less: Admin., Selling and Distribution	6.2	6.5	12.3	19.8
Other indirect expenses	1.4	1.4	1.7	2.8
Net Profit Before Tax	16.0	29.0	46.0	78.0
Return on Capital			43.4%	46.3%

Notes: 1. Net of grants and depreciation.
      2. Base stock 6 weeks; W.I.P. 3 weeks; F.G. 12 weeks.
      3. 8 weeks of net sales as Exhibit 5.
      4. 6 weeks of direct materials as Exhibit 5.
      5. As Exhibit 5.

8 Engineering Products Ltd

In 1976 Engineering Products Limited (EPL) was a diversified manufacturer of technically advanced equipment. In most of the fields in which the company operated it had a reputation as a leader, in terms of the design, quality and performance characteristics of its products, its delivery policies and its after-sales service policies. Users of its equipment generally considered EPL's products to be highly priced relative to competing products, but justifiable in terms of greater reliability in subsequent service. EPL had never, as a matter of policy, relied upon pricing as a major factor in its marketing efforts.

RECENT DEVELOPMENT OF THE COMPANY

Some selected statistics relating to the company's operations are shown below in £000's:

	1975	1974	1973	1972	1971
Operations			(£'000)		
Turnover	22,448	17,670	13,377	11,909	10,337
Net Profit	1,689	1,229	545	805	407
Financial Condition					
Working Capital	6,789	4,805	4,444	3,232	3,069
Fixed Assets (net)	16,488	11,649	7,335	5,826	4,721
Long-term Debt	10,922	7,664	4,609	2,957	2,373
Shareholders' Investment	10,347	7,852	6,802	6,352	5,641
Other Statistics					
Capital Expenditures	5,851	5,229	1,736	1,758	643
Dividends Paid	94	94	94	94	112
No. of Shareholders	476	377	291	193	135

During 1973 EPL had undergone a reorganisation of its management structure. Concurrently, a major commitment had been made to future growth; the planning slogan adopted by the company at that time, and still in use in 1976, was 'Growth for the Future'. A four-year plan had been devised which was intended to strengthen the company's production capabilities, using already demonstrated engineering expertise, and to prepare the company for major markets which it was thought would develop during the 1970s, and early 1980s. EPL was gearing its R & D, production facilities and products to proven growth markets, such as air transportation, power generation, mass urban transportation, and desalination of sea water. The common theme rationalising EPL's interest in these seemingly diverse markets lay in production and engineering skills; for example, expertise in producing and machining materials for service under extreme operating conditions of stress, pressure or temperature.

The company's management had chosen to base its growth on internal development of products and capabilities. Acquisitions and mergers had been considered as a means of growth and diversification, but had been rejected in favour of internal development. Management considered that it already had ample opportunities for using the company's capital without looking for acquisition opportunities.

Prepared from published data disguised to prevent identification of the actual firm.

FUTURE PLANS

EPL was continuing with its expansion programme which had been formulated in
1973. The following quotation is an excerpt from the chairman's statement which
accompanied the company's financial report for year ending June 30 1975

> Inflation is now running at about 25 per cent and must be tackled by all of us,
> government, employers and employees alike, as a matter of urgency. For our part we
> intend to pursue our investment for growth. . . . Capital expenditure of approxi-
> mately £8 million allowing for inflation are planned in each of the next two years.
> Funds will be provided by cash flow and by a £5 million long-term loan from an
> insurance company. The loan amount will be advanced in 1976, and in the
> meantime short-term bank loans have been arranged.

ATTACHED DATA

Extracts from the 1975 annual report are attached, including the balance sheet,
Exhibit 1, the profit and loss account, Exhibit 2, and the funds statement, Exhibit 3.
Some of the footnotes are shown as Exhibit 4. Exhibit 5 shows some indices as of the
same date, particularly showing the price index and the price earnings ratio of publicly
quoted firms in selected industries.

QUESTIONS FOR DISCUSSION

(1) Evaluate the performance of EPL to date.
(2) Prepare projected balance sheets, profit and loss accounts, and funds statement
    as far forward as you feel you can.
(3) Analyse the prospects for the company.
(4) Place a value on the entire share capital of the company.

EXHIBIT 1   Engineering Products Limited

Consolidated Balance Sheets as at June 30 1975 and 1974
£000's

Assets Employed	1975	1974
Fixed Assets		
Plant, Property and Equipment	22151	16340
Less provision for depreciation	5663	4691
	16488	11649
Investments	46	46
Other Assets	1407	647
	17941	12342
Current Assets		
Stocks and Work-in-progress	9578	6472
Debtors	3438	2456
Prepayments	481	90
Cash in bank and on deposit	251	608
	13748	9626
less *Current Liabilities*		
Bank overdraft and long term debts due	4398	1904
Creditors and accruals	2512	1833
Taxation	49	1084
	6959	4821
Net Working Capital	6789	4805
	24730	17147
Financed by:		
Ordinary Share Capital; Authorised 6,150,000 shares at 20p Issued 6,000,000 shares	1200	1200
Capital surplus	900	–
Capital and revenue reserves	8247	6652
Ordinary Shareholders Funds	10347	7852
Long term debt	10922	7664
Deferred Taxation	3461	1631
	24730	17147

EXHIBIT 2 Engineering Products Limited

Consolidated Profit and Loss Account and Appropriation Account for Years Ended June 30 1975 and 1974
£000's

	1975	1974
Sales Revenue	22448	17670
Costs and Expenses:		
Cost of Products sold	14146	11489
Selling, General and Administrative Expenses	3579	2992
Interest	1261	635
Other Deductions (income) net	(57)	(6)
	18929	15110
Profit Before Tax	3519	2560
Taxation (52%)	1830	1331
Profit After Tax	1689	1229
Reserves Brought Forward	6652	5348
Extraordinary Gains (net)	–	169
Dividends Declared and Paid	(94)	(94)
Reserves Carried Forward	8247	6652

EXHIBIT 3 Engineering Products Limited

Statement of Consolidated Source and Use of Funds for Years Ended 30 June 1975 and 1974
£000's

	1975	1974
Funds were provided by:		
Operations:		
Profit after tax	1689	1229
Depreciation	1126	825
Amortisation	26	–
Deferred Tax	1830	1331
	4671	3385
Increase in long term debt	3258	3055
Extraordinary gains (net)	–	169
	7929	6609
Funds were used for:		
Additions to plant, equipment and other assets	5851	5229
Payment of dividends	94	94
	5945	5323
Net Increase in Working Capital	1984	1268

EXHIBIT 4   Engineering Products Limited

Excerpts from Notes to the Financial Statements

Note 3.   The parent Holding Company refinanced its long-term debt to an insurance company under an agreement dated 1 November 1974. Under the terms of this agreement, the Company has drawn £7,000,000 up to 30 June 1975 and may borrow additional amounts of £2,500,000 in March 1976 and £2,500,000 in September 1976. The total debt to be issued (£12,000,000) is due 1 December 1995, with required annual prepayments of £400,000 in fiscal years 1978 to 1983, £500,000 from 1984 to 1987, £600,000 from 1988 to 1991 and £1,120,000 from 1992 to 1996. The agreement contains various restrictions on the Company, including the following: (*a*) other debt of the Parent Holding Company may not exceed £6,800,000 prior to 1 March 1976, £4,300,000 to 2 September 1976 and £1,800,000 thereafter; (*b*) working capital may not be less than £4,000,000 after September 1976; and (*c*) no limitation on payments of cash dividends from revenue reserves.

On 7 December 1974 authorised common shares of the Company were increased by 150,000 shares in connection with this new loan agreement. The Company gave the insurance company the right to purchase these 150,000 shares at £7.50 per share, this right being exercisable by the insurance company at any time prior to 1 December 1989. Upon the advice of a merchant bank, the Company has determined that £900,000 of the proceeds of the loan is applicable to this right to purchase shares. This amount has been reported as another asset (to be amortised as loan expense over the life of the loan) and as capital surplus in the balance sheet.

Note 4.   The debt of subsidiary companies, which is not included in the restrictions under the agreement with the insurance company except in so far as such debt is guaranteed by the Parent Holding Company, but which is secured by substantially all the assets of the subsidiary companies is as follows:

Loan from Funds for Industry to be repaid in semi-annual instalments of £112,000 beginning 30 June 1977, with an interest rate of 8%	£2,408,000
Ten per cent loan from the Funds For Industry, guaranteed by the Parent Holding Company, to be repaid in semi-annual instalments of £12,600 beginning 30 June 1977	252,000
Loans from the Newtown Development Corporation, bearing interest of 10%, to be repaid in semi-annual instalments over a 15-year period beginning 1 June 1975	950,000
Loan from a German bank (7% interest), guaranteed by the Parent Holding Company; £92,000 to be paid by 30 June 1976, £30,000 to be paid by 30 June 1977, and the remainder in four equal annual instalments thereafter.	212,000
Others, guaranteed by the Parent Holding Company.	66,400
	£3,889,000
Due within one year	161,800
	£3,727,000

Note 5.   (*a*) Taxation charges and deferments are as follows (£000)

	1975	*1974*
Charge for the year:		
Corporation tax at 52%	1830	1331
less deferred taxation available:		
initial capital allowance	3101	2714
stock appreciation relief	718	387
plus net change in A.C.T.	0	0
tax allowances not used	1989	1770

(*b*) Tax allowances not used may be carried forward but not backwards.

(*c*) Initial allowances for capital expenditure on plant and equipment are available such that 100% of the asset cost may be charged against taxable profit in the first year.

(*d*) Stock application relief is available as follows:

the increase in stock value over the financial year may be charged against taxable income, except that the increased stock value must first be reduced by 15% of the taxable income for the year (after capital allowances have been deducted therefrom.)

(*e*) No further capital investment allowances or incentives are available as EPL is not situated in a development area.

Note 6. Capital commitments for 1976 are as follows:

(£000)

1976

Contracted

5000

Authorised

but not

contracted

3000

EXHIBIT 5

Indices from the Financial Times 30 June 1975

	Price Index		*Price Earnings Ratio*
	Today	*Year Ago*	
Electricals	202	171	7.9
Heavy Engineering	132	98	5.8
General Engineering	96	74	6.4
Machine Tools	41	33	12.3
Electronics, Radio	91	93	6.6
All Industrials	118	100	7.4

9 Fudge Creations Ltd

Jonathan Burke, a recent graduate from a reputable school of business, had been appointed assistant to the chairman of Fudge Creations Ltd in May 1974. The company was of above average size for the specialist confectionary business in its region, and was engaged in the manufacture and wholesale distribution of high-quality, high-priced fudge. The company's founder and chairman, Armando Morrazoni, described himself as a creative confectioner, and had also proved himself to be an able businessman by building the company from scratch to its present size (see financial statements, Exhibits 1 and 2) in 18 years. Fifteen hundred employees were attached to the firm at the end of 1973, more than half of them women. The company was the town's biggest employer of female labour. Ample work was available for men, but there were few alternatives for women.

PRODUCTION

The production process for making fudge consisted of four stages. First, there was the mixing of the ingredients according to a formula about which Mr Morrazoni was extremely secretive. He would never let anyone else help him at this stage in the process, except that he had the bulkier ingredients loaded mechanically into the mixer.

The second stage was the baking process, which transformed the lumps of ingredients into a smooth, almost liquid substance, which upon cooling solidified slowly into fudge. The procedure was automatic and involved care only as regards the cooking time.

The third stage (called the finishing stage) was a creative process. Two foremen and 512 helpers were employed in 1973 in the conversion of the cooked fudge into a great variety of final products. This might involve *shaping* the fudge, perching a walnut or other item on top (called *topping*), *embedding* a cherry or other centre in the fudge, coating the fudge with chocolate, or some other operation which Morrazoni thought would enhance the sales appeal of the fudge.

The last stage involved *packaging and distribution*, which was very similar in all respects to packaging operations in other consumer goods business.

MECHANISATION

The operations in stage three, the finishing stage, had recently been partially mechanised. Just after the end of the last fiscal year ending 28 February 1974, Mr Morrazoni had taken delivery of 27 Markowitz 'Sweetsetter' machines. These machines could be used to perform the operations of topping, embedding, coating, and shape-cutting at great speeds. While only a single one of these operations could be done per run on a given machine, any fudge requiring several processes could simply be passed through several separate machines, each set to carry out one of the tasks.

As the capacities of the mixing, cooking and packaging departments were very much larger than the pre-mechanisation capacity of the finishing department, Mr Morrazoni thought the extra speed to be a great advantage. He also stated that he had purchased some extra machines to allow flexibility in manufacturing. Even though a smaller number of machines than the 27 purchased could have finished the current year's fudge production, he would not have considered such a purchase feasible, as he felt it would have been far too restrictive on his creativity. In Mr Morrazoni's opinion, the additional capacity of the spare machines simply *had* to be available. The department worked 250 eight-hour days a year, and remained, after mechanisation, the bottleneck in the production process, of all the departments.

With the new sweetsetters it had been possible to reduce the staff in the finishing department to two men for each machine, and two foremen. The hand-workers who had been employed previous to the purchase of the Markowitz machines were classed by the industry as Grade III workers, which entitled them to a wage rate of £0.96 per hour including fringe benefits. The union regulations required that two Grade III men be employed for each Markowitz machine, whether it was in use or not. It had also been necessary to employ two skilled set-up mechanics, at a total cost of £15,000 per annum, in order to prepare the machines for running by Grade III personnel who had previously done the hand-work. Redundancy pay had been paid to the men and women laid off, the cost of which had aggregated £1,435,100.

FINANCES

In addition to the debt outstanding on 28 February 1974, Mr Morrazoni had borrowed £350,000 at 13 per cent to help pay for the Markowitz machines. He had decided not to try to place equity. A small parcel of shares had recently changed hands at £625 each. This price reflected the small number of shares outstanding, only 10,000, and the stable dividend of £40 per share that had been paid for several years. Mr Morrazoni did not wish to reduce his own holding below 53 per cent of the equity, and Mr Burberry, a banker and large shareholder, had used up most of his spare cash in buying the small parcel.

MR BURKE'S PROPOSAL

Jonathan Burke had been told to familiarise himself with the industry and the plant in his early days with the company, and one of the ways he had set about doing this was by studying the trade journals. Looking through the advertisements in one issue, he noticed another machine for finishing confectionery, which looked most promising.

This machine was called the Horman 'Carve-o-Set'. This performed the same basic job as the Markowitz 'Sweetsetter' but was very much faster, and required only one attendant, although this attendant had to have a Grade II classification according to union regulations. Grade II workers were entitled to £1.45 per hour including fringe benefits.

The detailed specification of the machines are given in Exhibit 4. The two set-up men could handle the Horman machine as well as the Markowitz.

Burke went to Mr Morrazoni to ask permission for time to investigate the relative merits of the machines. Mr Morrazoni agreed, saying that it would be 'good practice for him' and that he 'had nothing important to be done at the moment anyway'. He considered that the subject was of little importance now, however, in view of the very recent investment in Markowitz machines, which had scarcely been used, and on which no depreciation had yet been charged. Although Burke was somewhat discouraged by this dubious approval of what he thought was a most significant project, he set about preparation of a statement of the costs of operations of the machines for Mr Morrazoni's consideration.

The corporation tax rules in 1974 were essentially on a cash flow basis. In addition to the revenue and expense items normally taxable, the rules allowed 100 per cent of the cost of capital items to be deducted in the year they were bought. Conversely, because of the particular circumstances of Fudge Creations Ltd the full proceeds obtained for any assets sold was added to taxable income for the year of the sale.

QUESTIONS

1. Was Mr Morrazoni right in installing the Markowitz machines? Define what you mean by 'right' in answering the question.
2. What is your verdict, after having compared the two machines? What should happen next? Why?

EXHIBIT 1   Fudge Creations Ltd

Profit and Loss Account, Year ended 28 February 1974

Sales (174, 681 gross)		£6,412,259
Discounts allowed		1,026,687
		£5,385,672
Materials (net of scrap)	£ 590,453	
Labour	1,742,581	
Factory Expenses	1,047,321	
		3,380,355
		£2,005,317
General, Selling and Administrative		805,513
Profit before tax		£1,199, 804

EXHIBIT 2   Fudge Creations Ltd

Summary Balance Sheet as at 28 February 1974

Current Assets	£2,516,527
Current Liabilities	1,247,625
Working Capital	£1,268,902
Fixed Assets	5,623,317
	£6,892,219
Long-term liabilities	2,500,000
Net Worth	£4,392,219

EXHIBIT 3   Fudge Creations Ltd

Total Sales of Fudge within the Region, and Sales by Fudge Creations Ltd, in numbers of Gross of Packages

	Total Sales	Fudge Creation Sales
1973	2,001,833	174,681
1972	2,317,966	200,547
1971	2,564,321	222,341
1970	2,879,628	249,668
1969	3,048,217	262,315
1968	3,064,283	247,385
1967	2,982,137	232,174
1966	2,768,546	221,897
1965	2,677,122	166,358
1964	2,720,332	153,221

Note: A gross of packages means 144 one pound boxes of fudge, or twice that number of half pound boxes, etc.

EXHIBIT 4
Machine Specifications

All figures refer to one machine of each type

	Markowitz	Horman
Cost to purchase	£16,500	£106,000
Operatives required	2	1
Maximum Output, in gross/hour	4	17
Intended retention period in years	5	5
Anticipated average annual preventive maintenance cost	£ 700	£ 4,950
Power cost/year	£ 8,050	£ 14,700
Supplies needed/year	600	£ 2,000
Second hand market price	£11,000	£ 89,000

Note: The second-hand market prices of these and other similar machines have been subject to acute fluctuations. At present they are very high, as shown, but they are often near zero depending on demand.

EXHIBIT 5 Fudge Creations Ltd

Expenses analysed by departments for the year to 28 February 1974

	Mixing Department	Banking Department	Finishing Department	Packing Department	Total	
Direct materials	391,354		143,186	97,466		632,006
Direct Labour (machinists)	265,060	249,408	12,306	71,386	598,160	
(hand workers)	–	16,004	859,994	93,897	969,895	
Indirect labour	13,412	12,716	31,834	7,664	65,626	
Fringe benefits	17,352	18,111	62,335	11,102	108,900	
	295,824	296,239	966,469	184,049		1,742,581
Power	23,310	30,664	7,459	14,328	75,761	
Supplies	16,615	11,132	18,282	2,151	48,180	
Repairs	53,612*	12,312	564	1,328	67,816	
Depreciation of machines	122,000	109,000	1,350	41,000	273,350	
	215,537	163,108	27,655	58,807		465,107
Light and Heat	7,126	6,683	11,215	4,598	29,622	
Building Services	12,315	11,777			24,092	
Rent			168,300	71,200	239,500	
Depreciation of Buildings	152,000	137,000			289,000	
	171,441	155,460	179,515	75,798		582,214
General	127,000	141,000	102,000	12,000	382,000	
Interest	58,000	49,000	1,001	32,070	140,071	
Expenses				283,442	283,442	
	185,000	190,000	103,001	327,512		805,513
	1,259,156	804,807	1,419,826	743,632		4,227,421
Less – scrap sales etc.	34,372		7,181			41,553
	1,224,784	804,807	1,412,645	743,632		4,185,868

* This amount includes fire damage of £37,260.

10 Hanson Manufacturing Company

In February 1955, Mr Herbert Wessling was appointed general manager by Mr Paul Hanson, president of the Hanson Manufacturing Company. Mr Wessling, age fifty-six, had wide executive experience in manufacturing products similar to those of the Hanson company. The appointment of Mr Wessling resulted from management problems arising from the death of Mr Richard Hanson, founder and, until his death in early 1954, president of the Hanson company. Mr Paul Hanson had only four years' experience with the company, and in early 1955 was thirty-four years old. His father had hoped to train him over a ten-year period, but his untimely death had cut this seasoning period short. The younger Hanson became president when his father died and had exercised full control until he hired Mr Wessling.

Mr Paul Hanson knew that during 1954 he had made several poor decisions and noted that the morale of the organisation had suffered, apparently through lack of confidence in him. When he received the profit and loss statement for 1954 (Exhibit 1), the net loss of over $51,000 during a good business year convinced him that he needed help. He attracted Mr Wessling from a competitor by offering a stock option incentive in addition to salary, knowing that Mr Wessling wanted to acquire a financial competence for his retirement. The two men came to a clear understanding that Mr Wessling, as general manager, had full authority to execute any changes he desired. In addition, Mr Wessling would explain the reasons for his decisions to Mr Hanson and thereby train him for successful leadership upon Mr Wessling's retirement.

The Hanson Manufacturing Company made only three industrial products, 101, 102, and 103. These were sold by company salesmen for use in the processes of other manufacturers. All of the salesmen, on a salary basis, sold the three products but in varying proportions. The Hanson company sold throughout New England and was one of eight companies with similar products. Several of its competitors were larger and manufactured a larger variety of products than did the Hanson company. The dominant company was the Samra Company, which operated a branch plant in the Hanson company's market area. Customarily, the Samra Company announced prices annually, and the other producers followed suit.

Price cutting was rare, and the only variance from quoted selling prices took the form of cash discounts. In the past, attempts at price cutting had followed a consistent pattern: all competitors met the price reduction, and the industry as a whole sold about the same quantity but at the lower prices. This continued until the Samra Company, with its strong financial position, again stabilised the situation following a general recognition of the failure of price cutting. Furthermore, because sales were to industrial buyers and because the products of different manufacturers were very similar, the Hanson Company was convinced it could not individually raise prices without suffering volume declines.

During 1954 the Hanson company's share of industry sales was 12 per cent for type 101, 8 per cent for 102, and 10 per cent for 103. The industry-wide quoted selling prices were $2.45, $2.58, and $2.75, respectively.

Mr Wessling, upon taking office in February 1955, decided against immediate major changes. Rather he chose to analyse 1954 operations and to wait for results of the first half of 1955. He instructed the accounting department to provide detailed expenses and earnings statements by products for 1954 (see Exhibit 2). In addition he requested an explanation of the nature of the costs including their expected future behaviour (see Exhibit 3).

To familiarise Mr Paul Hanson with his methods, Mr Wessling sent copies of these exhibits to Mr Hanson, and they discussed them. Mr Hanson stated that he thought Product 103 should be dropped immediately as it would be impossible to lower expenses on Product 103 as much as 22 cents per cwt. In addition he stressed the need for economies on Product 102.

Mr Wessling relied on the authority arrangement Mr Hanson had agreed to earlier and continued production of the three products. For control purposes he had the accounting department prepare monthly statements using as standard costs the costs per cwt from the analytical profit and loss statement for 1954 (Exhibit 2). These monthly statements were his basis for making minor sales or production changes during the spring of 1955. Late in July 1955, Mr Wessling received from the accounting department the six months' statement of cumulative standard costs including variances of actual costs from standard (see Exhibit 4). They showed that the first half of 1955 was a successful period.

During the latter half of 1955 the sales of the entire industry weakened. Even though the Hanson company retained its share of the market, its profit for the last six months was small. In January 1956, the Samra Company announced a price reduction on Product 101 from $2.45 to $2.25 per cwt. This created an immediate pricing problem for all its competitors. Mr Wessling forecast that if the Hanson company held to the $2.45 price during the first six months 1956, their unit sales would be 750,000 cwt. He felt that if they dropped their price to $2.25 per cwt the six months' volume would be 1,000,000 cwt. Mr Wessling knew that competing managements anticipated a further decline in activity. He thought a general decline in prices was quite probable.

The accounting department reported that the standard costs in use would probably apply during 1956, with two exceptions: materials and supplies would be about 5 per cent below standard; and light and heat would decline about one third of 1 per cent.

Mr Wessling and Mr Hanson discussed the pricing problem. Mr Hanson observed that even with the anticipated decline in material and supply costs, a sales price of $2.25 would be below cost. Mr Hanson therefore wanted the $2.45 price to be continued since he felt the company could not be profitable while selling a key product below cost.

QUESTIONS

1. Was Mr Wessling correct in his decision not to drop Product 103 in the spring of 1955
2. In January 1956, should the company have reduced the price of Product 101 from $2.45 to $2.25 or to an intermediate figure?

EXHIBIT 1 Hanson Manufacturing Company

Profit and Loss Statement for Year ending 31 December 1954

Gross sales			$ 10,589,405
Cash discount			156,578
Net sales			10,432,827
Cost of manufacturing			$ 7,411,038
Manufacturing profit			$ 3,021,789
Less: Selling expense	$ 1,838,238		
General administration	653,020		
Depreciation	458,440		2,949,698
Operating profit			$ 72,091
Other income			21,065
Net profit before bond interest			$ 93,156
Less: Interest on bonds			145,083
Net Loss after All Charges			$ 51,927

EXHIBIT 2 Hanson Manufacturing Company

Analysis of Profit and Loss by Departments – Year ended 31 December 1954

	Product 101		Product 102		Product 103		Total	Direct	Allocated	Basis of Allocation
	Thousands	$ per cwt.	Thousands	$ per cwt.	Thousands	$ per cwt.	Thousands			
Rent	187	.0881	157	.1525	188	.1894	532		X	Cubic Space Used
Property Taxes	62	.0293	50	.0485	40	.0405	152		X	Area
Property Insurance	52	.0245	40	.0387	53	.0533	145		X	Value of equip.
Compensation Insurance	83	.0387	43	.0422	45	.0455	171	X		Direct labour $
Direct Labour	1293	.6063	610	.5922	687	.6965	2590		X	Direct labour $
Indirect Labour	441	.2068	212	.2058	230	.2330	883		X	Machine HP
Power	22	.0105	25	.0242	30	.0305	77		X	Area
Light & Heat	15	.0070	13	.0123	10	.0102	38		X	Area
Building Service	10	.0047	8	.0075	7	.0075	25		X	
Materials	764	.3585	471	.4576	485	.4912	1720	X		
Supplies	52	.0245	48	.0462	35	.0355	135	X		
Repairs	18	.0083	15	.0145	10	.0103	43	X		
Total	2999	1.4072	1692	1.6422	1820	1.8434	6511			
Selling Expense	910	.4270	458	.4445	470	.4762	1838		X	$ value of sale
General Administrative	345	.1617	130	.1263	178	.1798	653		X	$ value of sale
Depreciation	565	.2649	427	.4155	365	.3704	1357		X	Value of equip.
Interest	52	.0245	40	.0388	53	.0532	145		X	Value of equip.
Total Cost	4871	2.2853	2747	2.6673	2886	2.9230	10504			
Less Other Income	10	.0048	5	.0050	5	.0050	20		X	$ value of sale
	4861	2.2605	2742	2.6623	2881	2.9180	10484			
Sales (net)	5167	2.4235	2599	2.5228	2667	2.7027	10433			
Profit or Loss	306	.1430	143*	.1395*	214*	.2153*	51*			
Unit Sales (cwt.)	2132191		1029654		986974					
Quoted Selling Price	$2.45		$2.58		$2.75					
Cash Discounts taken % (of selling price)	1.08%		2.03%		1.72%		1.48%			

* Loss

Note – figures may not check exactly because of rounding.

EXHIBIT 3 Hanson Manufacturing Company

Accounting Department's Commentary on Costs

Direct Labour: Variable. Union shop at going community rates of $1.60/hr. No abnormal demands foreseen. It may be assumed that direct labour dollars is an adequate measure of capacity utilization.

Compensation Insurance: Variable. Five per cent of direct and indirect labour is an accurate estimate.

Materials: Variable. Exhibit 2 figures are accurate. Includes waste allowances. Purchase are at market prices.

Power: Variable. Rates are fixed. Use varies with activity. Averages per Exhibit 2 are accurate.

Supplies: Variable. Exhibit 2 figures are accurate. Supplies bought at market prices.

Repairs: Variable. Varies as volume changes within normal operation range. Lower and upper limits are fixed.

General Administrative, Selling Expense, Indirect Labour, Interest, and Other Income: These items are almost non-variable. They can be changed, of course by management decision.

Cash Discount: Almost non-variable. Average cash discounts taken are consistent from year to year. Percentages in Exhibit 2 are accurate.

Light and Heat: Almost non-variable. Heat varies slightly with fuel cost changes. Light a fixed item regardless of level of production.

Property Taxes: Almost non-variable. Under the lease terms Hanson company pays the taxes; assessed valuation has been constant; the rate has risen slowly. Any change in the near future will be small and independent of production volume.

Rent: Non-variable. Lease has twelve years to run.

Building Service: Non-variable. At normal business level variances are small.

Property Insurance: Non-variable. Three-year policy with fixed premium.

Depreciation: Non-variable. Fixed dollar total.

EXHIBIT 4 Hanson Manufacturing Company

Profit and Loss by Department, at Standard, Showing variations from 1 January to 30 June 1955

Item	Product 101 Standard per cwt.	Product 101 Total at Standard	Product 102 Standard per cwt.	Product 102 Total at Standard	Product 103 Standard per cwt.	Product 103 Total at Standard	Total Standard (Thousands)	Total Actual (Thousands)	Variations + = Favourable − = Unfavourable
Rent	.0881	88	.1525	110	.1894	96	294	261	+ 33
Property Tax	.0293	29	.0485	35	.0405	20	84	77	+ 7
Property Insurance	.0245	25	.0387	28	.0533	27	80	73	+ 7
Compensation Insurance	.0387	39	.0422	30	.0455	23	92	92	
Direct Labour	.6063	604	.5922	422	.6965	349	1375	1382	− 7
Indirect Labour	.2068	206	.2058	147	.2330	117	470	448	+ 22
Power	.0105	10	.0242	17	.0305	15	42	42	
Light and Heat	.0070	7	.0123	9	.0102	5	21	20	+ 1
Building Service	.0047	5	.0075	5	.0075	4	14	10	+ 4
Materials	.3585	357	.4576	326	.4912	246	929	928	+ 1
Supplies	.0245	24	.0462	33	.0355	18	75	75	
Repairs	.0083	8	.0145	10	.0103	5	23	25	− 2
Total	1.4072	1402	1.6422	1172	1.8434	925	3499	3433	+ 66
Selling Expense	.4270	426	.4445	317	.4762	239	982	983	− 1
General Administrative	.1617	161	.1263	90	.1798	90	341	328	+ 13
Depreciation	.2649	264	.4155	294	.3704	185	743	681	+ 62
Interest	.0245	25	.0388	28	.0532	26	79	73	+ 6
Total Cost	2.2853	2278	2.6673	1901	2.9230	1465	5644	5498	+ 146
Less Other Income	.0048	5	.0050	3	.0050	2	10	11	+ 1
Actual Sales	2.2805	2273	2.6623	1898	2.9180	1463	5634	5487	+ 147
	2.4235	2416	2.5228	1796	2.7027	1355	5567	5567	
Profit or loss	.1430	143	.1395*	102*	.2153*	108*	67*	80	+ 147
Unit Sales	996859		712102		501276				

11 James & Breasley Ltd (A)

BACKGROUND

James and Breasley Limited is a well-known name in the West Country. Its incorporation dates back to 1876, and its products have both a national and international reputation. When these products pass through its gates, they are usually very large and require special transportation, and many of the locals stand by to watch. The company is engaged in heavy constructional engineering production, with the emphasis between the turn of the century and immediately before the Second World War on bridges, but with the current emphasis on a wide range of products, including constructional work for nationalised undertakings, such as the United Kingdom Atomic Energy Authority.

Much of the factory premises date back to the early 1900s and although the design and drawing office has a clinical-looking new block, the original office, a Victorian house, still accommodates three members of top management and the accounting department. The various production and service departments in the factory house 800 employees, many of whom have worked for the company since leaving school, and whose fathers and grandfathers worked there before them. In some production departments, there are still family groups. All in all, this has been a business run by a benevolent management, given only in recent years to a few and limited redundancies. These have been occasioned by recessions in this very difficult and competitive market. The company has been cushioned to some extent by its reputation and special expertise, and in particular, by its ability to meet delivery dates much better than its competitors. Often this has been a costly procedure, but the company has never failed to make a profit in a trading year, in spite of one or two near-misses in recent years, when the return on investment has been very low.

The financial director of the company, a Scot, has in his five years with the company done much to inculcate among top management a better idea of financial objectives, and has reorganised, with the enthusiastic assistance of two subordinates, a company secretary and a chief accountant, the whole of the financial accounting, from basic ledgers to quarterly financial statements. He has not found it necessary to devote as much energy to the product costing side of the business, which he considered to be quite well developed when he joined the company. This product costing follows traditional job costing procedures. Each contract receives a job number followed by job part numbers to which direct materials and components, direct labour and direct expenses are booked through bills of material and material requisitions, wage tickets and time sheets, and in some cases direct from invoices, cash-book and petty cash-book. The factory is divided into departments, each with a departmental number, and any part of prime cost booked to job numbers is identifiable with the factory department in which the expenditure is incurred.

DEPARTMENTAL OVERHEAD RATES

Each department has its own overhead rate, which includes departmental, factory general, administration, selling and distribution expenses. The departmental overhead rates are re-calculated annually on the basis of budgeted labour costs and overheads for each department. A little disturbing to the financial director has been the fact that the departments are factory locations, and in a sense budget centres also, but

Reprinted from *Management Accounting*, June 1971.

each department contains several different operations, involving the use of different plant, equipment and facilities. He senses that a very good argument could be raised for using different overhead rates for each operation, but he fears the amount of cost analysis which would be necessary to achieve this. On the other hand, the present system has anomalies since the same operation is in some cases carried out in three different factory departments and carries, as a result, three different overhead rates.

COMPLETION OF CONTRACTS

A particular problem with which the financial director, Milne, has had to grapple, and which was quite new to him when he joined the company, has involved the attention of the chief accountant and the cost accountant. This is the problem of completions, which involves determining those contracts which can reasonably be regarded as complete at the end of a trading period, and for which credit can be taken for the sales income and the profit on the contract, if any. The decisions on this matter cannot be made on the basis of whether or not the job has left the factory premises; but whether it is felt from correspondence with the customer, or evidence from the representative on the site, that the product is to the customer's satisfaction, and whether there is any likelihood of any additional work or rectification which might involve James and Breasley in additional costs.

DEPARTMENTAL BUDGETARY CONTROL

Some 18 months ago, Milne turned his attention to budgetary control. He had worked in Scotland for a business, in an entirely different line of trade, which had well-developed budgetary control procedures, and he was convinced that these resulted in top management obtaining a better involvement in performance and cost control of all managers in the business, right down to supervisors on the shop floor. He was determined to get such procedures instituted in James and Breasley, and to this end promoted the best clerk in the cost office to budget officer. This young man, 23 years of age, Peter Franks, was reckoned to be a good prospect. He was already studying for a professional qualification, had a pleasing personality and was very acceptable to everyone in the organisation, having worked there since leaving school. Milne had some doubt concerning Franks' ability to be firm when it was necessary, and this was a matter which he discussed with Franks very fully when he gave him his terms of reference. 'Installing budgetary control procedures is going to be a slow process. I want you to start at departmental, shop floor level so that as soon as possible we can involve the interest of departmental supervisors and their immediate superiors, the factory superintendents and so on up to the works manager. It's not going to be easy to involve the works manager. He's definitely anti-accounting, and in any conversations that I've had with him, he has been most unhappy about the idea that anyone below his level should receive control information. When we start producing control information, you must take upon yourself the role of presenter and interpreter, pointing out where things are going wrong, and this will mean you'll have to be firm and persistent. We will start slowly, on the basis of what we have already, that is a departmental analysis of costs produced mainly to facilitate the re-calculation of overhead recovery rates. Build on that. I'm not expecting miracles.'

Peter Franks got moving. Existing financial and cost accounting procedures threw up a detailed analysis of costs, in a piecemeal fashion, which he could bring together to provide actual cost information for his departmental operating statements. His first shot at departmental budgets was carried out with some aid from production department supervisors, but consisted mainly of historical cost data. From the start he was worried about the setting of the level of activity. In fact, he was not even sure that activity could be measured in a realistic manner. In a few shops the production was reasonably standard and operators were paid on a piecework basis. But in most shops the work was one-off or small batch production, involving no piecework payments, and the only information available was the time booked to individual jobs and part numbers. His first thoughts were that in these circumstances the level of activity could only be assessed on the basis of actual direct hours worked or in relationship to direct wages. In any case, he did not see how he could start on flexible departmental budgets; he decided, in view of Milne's comments, that he would adopt a fixed budget approach, comparing actual costs of actual activity with the budgeted costs for the budgeted activity. It concerned him that departmental costing already existed to facilitate the calculation of overhead rates, and that the managing director himself showed a great interest in the under- or over-absorption of overheads. He felt that it should be possible to combine departmental budgetary control with a calculation each period of this under- or over-absorption of overheads.

Peter would have admitted to anyone that the first attempts were rough and ready, but he had made a start, and a typical departmental operating statement appears in Exhibit 2. At least, Peter felt, the one statement sufficed to give control information to departmental managers and supervisors, while at the same time providing the calculation of overhead recovery which the managing director was so keen to see each period. The actual overhead absorption of £6.442 is represented by the predetermined overhead rate of 375 per cent applied to the actual direct wages of £1,718.

It was at this stage that Stokes, a friend of the financial director, arrived. Stokes had given some assistance recently to the company in recruiting staff, and Milne wanted his advice on budgetary control, particularly with regard to Departmental Operating Statements.

After a detailed investigation on a part-time basis, Stokes sent the following memo to Milne:

Memo to Milne from Stokes Budgetary Control Procedures

My thoughts on the matter so far are:

1. Much of the present work which is done in a monthly accounting period is duplicatory. For example, general service and fixed costs are allocated and apportioned at the budget stage, and then the process is repeated each month on the basis of actual figures. Apart from being duplicatory, the results of this exercise are quite meaningless. This is very clear to the man who is doing the job and gives him little satisfaction.

2. The first task is to provide a clear division of the costs budgeted for individual departments into 'directly attributable controllable', 'directly attributable fixed', and 'general and fixed overheads apportioned'. In the long term there must be training of managers, foremen and the like, in order that they may all be involved in the budget setting. One would like to see them accepting the fullest responsibility for the 'directly attributable controllable' items.

I am not happy about what seems to be a complete lack of integration between the sales forecasting and shop floor manning which is built into the budget. Clearly, direct and indirect labour manning as contained in departmental budgets should be related to the budgeted level of activity, and I suggest that the level of activity can only be expressed in terms of the work content of individual jobs, orders and products. Further development in the measurement of departmental effectiveness will depend upon getting reliable measurements of work produced. The amount of work produced is not reflected by actual hours worked but by standard hours produced. I recommend that Franks should concentrate his attention on efficiency measurements in future, rather than on the present duplicatory clerical aspects of the budgetary control work.

3. I attach a proposed Departmental Operating Statement for a Production Department.[1] The particular points which I would like to stress about this are:

---

[1] See Exhibit 1.

(a) Operating Measures

In this section we highlight, both in budget and actual terms, normal as opposed to overtime operating hours, waiting time, and a calculation of the activity percentage against budget. I would like to think that the 'hours produced' figures might at some time in the future be standard hours produced'. It is not sufficient merely to think in terms of number of people. The manning must be converted into normal working hours, and decisions must be taken about the extent of overtime which will be required and permitted. A further decision will be required regarding the 'standard' at which overtime premium shall be set. It will be necessary to decide upon a 'standard' for waiting time, so that the total attendance hours can be scaled down to give a figure of budgeted productive hours.

(b) Directly Attributable / Controllable

I want to interest the departmental supervisor initially in the first section, 'directly attributable controllable', in which the original budget can be flexed on the basis of hours produced. Any difference between actual costs and the flexed budget we would have to call a 'spending variance', until we have the standard hours information which would enable us to calculate an 'efficiency variance'. You will notice that I am recommending a more detailed breakdown of direct and indirect labour cost items in this section. They are significant enough to warrant the detail.

(c) Directly Attributable / Fixed Overheads

The second section of cost items is concerned with overheads which, though fixed, are directly attributable to the department. These items of cost should be carefully budgeted at the beginning of the year and included in a 'Fixed Cost Budget' or, if appropriate, a series of 'Fixed Cost Budgets' which are under the command of particular directors or senior executives. They are not controllable in the departmental budget. In fact, the only reason for having them there is in order that a capacity variance on these costs can be established. I am suggesting that this capacity variance should be calculated each control period in the operating statement by comparing the overhead absorbed by the actual use of capacity with the original budget. I do not see the point in putting the actual costs against the original budget in this departmental operating statement. Incidentally, if we could agree not to be involved in the apportionment of cost items each control period, this would very considerably reduce the amount of clerical work. This clerical work is not justified because it does not assist shop floor control.

(d) General and Fixed Overheads

The third section of cost items is concerned with general, service and fixed overheads, which I suggest should be apportioned to each department at the budget stage on the basis of usage or potential usage; in other words, at an agreed standard. I am suggesting the same treatment for this section of costs as for the 'directly attributable fixed overheads', namely, that capacity variances only shall be calculated in the Production Department operating statement.

(e) Cost Variances

It is possible to show a figure on the operating statement of total variance, comprising spending and capacity. This is the only over- or under-recovery of cost for that department which can be calculated. Certainly cost variance information will be more meaningful than the overhead recovery information which was formerly provided on the operating statement. The next step must be to use standard hours produced which will allow us to compute efficiency variances. This will be relatively straightforward in one or two departments, but much more difficult in others, since this does represent a significant problem in performance measurement in jobbing situations.

The reader is now invited to appraise the comments and proposals of the consultant. The following questions are relevant:

(1) Is the revised Departmental Operating Statement an improvement? Can you suggest refinements?

(2) How can the company ensure that the operating statement is a key to effective and efficient management control?

(3) Should the company have concentrated its attention at this end of the budgetary control process?

EXHIBIT 1

DEPARTMENTAL OPERATING STATEMENT

Dept: MACHINE SHOP   *Supervisor*: J. R. MAY   *Period*: 15
No. of Wkg. Days: 20

OPERATING MEASURES

	Normal Op. Hours	*O/T Op. Hours*	*Total Op. Hours*	*Waiting Time*	*Net Prod. Hours*	*Hours Produced*
Budget	3,200	160	3,360	336	3,024	3,024
Actual	2,884	227	3,101	399	2,702	2,702

OPERATING COSTS

ACTIVITY %90

Directly Attributable Controllable	*Original Budget* *(wkg. days)*	*Flexed Budget Based on Hrs. Produced*	*Actual*	*Spending* *Over*	*Variance* *Under*	*Cum*
	£	£	£	£	£	
Direct Labour	1,700	1,530	1,582	52	—	
Direct Labour—O/T Prem.	30	27	43	16	—	
—Waiting Time	100	90	120	30	—	
Indirect Labour						
—Category "A"	355	320	347	27	—	
—Category "B"	106	96	102	6	—	
—O/T Prem.	50	45	45	—	—	
Associated Labour Costs						
—NHI/GP	65	59	63	4	—	
—Holiday pay	96	86	90	4	—	
—Insurance	20	18	19	1	—	
Process Materials	—	—	—	—	—	
Other Indirect Materials	200	180	200	20	—	
Coal, Coke & Oil	—	—	—	—	—	
Elec. & Gas Apportionment	126	113	100	—	13	
Repairs & Maintenance	340	306	242	—	64	
	3,188	2,870	2,953	160	77	

Directly Attributable Fixed Overheads	Original Budget	Actual Use of Capacity has Absorbed	Capacity Variance	
			Under	Over
Building Occupation	170			
Depreciation	330			
Salaries	125			
	625	563	62	—

General & Fixed Overheads Apportioned to Department	Original Budget	Actual Use of Capacity has Absorbed	Capacity Variance	
			Under	Over
Service	480			
Administration	520			
	1,000	900	100	

EXHIBIT 2

DEPARTMENTAL OPERATING AND BUDGET STATEMENT

Department: Pipe-making   *No.*: 34   *Period*: 7   *Month ending*: 27th Oct.

OPERATING STATISTICS

	This Momth	To Date		This Month	To Date
Budgeted direct hours	6,242	47,164	Budgeted direct wages	2,592	19,584
Actual direct hours worked	4,152	37,287	Actual direct wages	1,718	15,490
Capacity usage %	66.2	79.0	Direct wages variance	874	4,094
Pre-determined overhead %	375	375	Budgeted indirect/direct %	24.3	24.3
Actual overhead %	442	402	Actual indirect/direct %	30.4	34.0

OVERHEADS

	Code	This Month			Year To Date			Remarks
		Budget	Actual	Variance	Budget	Actual	Variance	
Direct Overheads								
Rent, Rates & Water		256	256	—	1,908	1,908	—	
Power, Light & Heat		1,336	1,533	(197)	8,358	8,829	(471)	
Sundry Shop Stores		16	6	10	122	75	47	
Repairs & Maintenance		1,264	931	333	9,547	10,204	(657)	
Shop Labour		629	523	106	4,759	5,269	(510)	
Process Materials		—	—	—	—	—	—	
NHI & Grad. Pension		187	234	(47)	1,414	1,430	(16)	
EL & PL Insurance		22	17	5	164	159	5	
Works Bonus		36	36	—	272	284	(12)	
Added Time		230	35	195	1,740	1,230	510	
Works Salaries		144	137	7	1-088	1,058	30	
Depreciation		364	364	—	2,748	2,748	—	
Holiday Pay		191	153	38	1,442	1,287	155	
		4,675	4,225	450	33,562	34,481	(919)	
Indirect Overheads								
Works Expenses		32	54	(22)	244	289	(45)	
Welfare		11	6	5	81	80	1	
Transport								
Admin. Salaries								
Admin. Charges								
Printing and Stationery								
Selling Expenses						7	(7)	
		43	66	(17)	325	376	(51)	

Allocated Overheads						
Works Services	1,355	1,616	(261)	10,833	12,679	(1,846)
Administration	1,669	1,394	275	12,347	13,393	(1,046)
Sales	402	388	14	3,038	3,042	(4)
General (Credits)	(138)	(85)	(53)	(1,041)	(1,547)	506
	3,288	3,313	(25)	25,177	27,567	(2,390)
Total Overheads:	8,006	7,598	408	59,064	62,424	(3,360)

Overhead Absorption:	Budget	8,006			59,064	
	Actual		6,442			58,080
Actual Overheads			7,598			62,424
Under-recovery			(1,156)			(4,344)

The reader is now invited to critically appraise the existing Departmental Operating Statement and consider possible improvements.

12 James & Breasley Ltd (B)

JAMES AND BREASLEY LTD, incorporated in 1876, is a well-known name in the West country; its products have a national and international reputation. These products are usually very large and require special transport so that as they pass through the gates locals often stand by to watch.

The company is in heavy constructional engineering production and the emphasis, between the turn of the century to immediately before the Second World War, was on bridges; now there is a wide range of products, including constructional work for nationalised undertakings, such as the United Kingdom Atomic Energy Authority.

Recently the company had been involved in developing budgeting control in their jobbing company.

DISAPPOINTING RESULTS

With the help of Stokes, a consultant friend, the chief accountant Milne had revised the departmental operating statements so that the points stressed were:

Operating measures;
Directly attributable/controllable expenses;
Directly attributable/fixed overheads;
General and fixed overheads;
Cost variances.

Milne was not satisfied with the results and had asked Stokes again for his advice. Milne explained that the exercise seemed to have involved little more than a re-arrangement of information and, apart from cutting out some duplication of effort, small benefit seemed to have been obtained; indeed, shop floor performance and control had not improved.

Stokes was disappointed at the lack of improvement and promised to investigate. After some weeks, he was able to report back.

In Stokes' opinion, the application of the change in the departmental budgeting system still had not taken sufficient account of a number of particular factors affecting the behaviour and attitudes of the managers and employees. These factors, evident at the time of the first report, were:

Many employees had worked for the company since leaving school; fathers and grandfathers had worked there before them and in some production departments there were still some closely knit family groups;
The works manager was unhappy about the idea that anyone below his level should receive control information and was clearly acting as a brakeman:
The chief accountant had worked in Scotland for a business which had well-developed budgetary control procedures but which operated in a different trade; in addition, Peter Franks, a young cost clerk had worked for the company since leaving school and had been promoted to budget officer.

TECHNICAL CHARACTERISTICS

There were a number of technical factors, particular to the company, which had not

Reprinted from *Management Accounting*, June 1971.

been fully appreciated either in the design or application of the system:

The company was engaged in heavy constructional engineering production on orders which, for the main part, had a long time cycle;

The market was highly competitive and the company had been cushioned to some extent by its technical reputation and special expertise and, in particular, by its ability to meet delivery dates much better than competitors;

It was extremely difficult to forecast in a realistic way the level of activity and to measure actual activity;

In most production shops the work was one-off or small batch and did not involve piecework payments.

EXISTING WEAKNESSES

Failure to appreciate to the full the implications of the social and technical factors had created certain weaknesses in the budgeting system:

The impression given to Stokes and other managers was that a text book standard costing system, which happened to work well in an entirely different business in Scotland, was being forced on to this jobbing company.

Departmental managers and employees represented highly cohesive groups which felt threatened by the emphasis of the new system and the way in which it had been implemented by the works manager: such cohesive groups with negative attitudes to the company represented a highly dangerous situation.

Negative attitudes had been engendered by the works manager's style of management; departmental managers were not joining in budget setting and the required standards of performance were imposed; some departmental heads considered that the budgets confirmed only what was already obvious and that they prevented supervisors from exercising real leadership.

The departmental operating statements were being used by the works manager to exact retribution; there was some evidence that some highly cohesive groups were intervening in the data processing system and that some unfavourable information was suppressed; for example, Stokes reported instances of scrapped work hidden in swarf bins or smuggled out to prevent the losses being recorded on the operating statement: some supervisors had justified this action by claiming that the budgets were misleading as a means of measuring performance because they did not explain why variations or excesses had occurred.

Emphasis in the departmental operating statements on the control of labour had lifted attention from the progress and control of individual jobs; since the labour cost percentage of total job cost was of the order of 20 per cent this emphasis could be misplaced.

Departmental managers were confused about the objectives of budgetary control: the relative inexperience of Peter Franks in attempting to push through a text book application of standard costing in an unsuitable situation, plus the management style of the works manager, had adversely affected attitudes.

Stokes had not been asked specifically to propose remedial action but he made suggestions to improve the situation.

First, he felt that there was a basic objective to design a budgetary control system which properly took into account the outstanding social and technical characteristics.

In dealing with the social factors, he thought that the departmental managers, the works manager and the chief accountant each had a different perception of the purpose of the budgeting system. Stokes recommended that the chief accountant should take immediate personal action to explain the objectives of the system, to review the ways in which the works manager involved departmental managers in budget setting and how he handled feedback of operating results.

Stokes further suggested that the negative attitude of the departmental managers should be studied. It might be necessary to remove the works manager unless he was prepared to change his style of management in line with the more participative approach which was being encouraged by the directors. The strong team spirit which still existed in departments should be channelled into activities favourable to the company.

CO-OPERATIVE BASIS

The focus of attention of the group should be turned away from the works manager and the departmental budgeting system to the job, its progress and costs. In view of the difficulty of measurement and the presence of strong groups, departments should be encouraged to manage their activities on a co-operative basis.

Positive attitudes should be encouraged in a variety of ways such as competitions, suggestion schemes with cash prizes, outings or holidays, or even direct financial incentives. Stokes contended that in this type of industry, flexibility and adaptability was required to deal with a wide range of jobs. The company had a major asset in the strong, informal groups in operating departments. The budgeting system should not misuse this valuable asset.

The reader is invited to consider how he would design and operate a control system, taking full account of the social and technical factors outlined in the case.

13 Manaus Woodpulp Corporation

The Investment Committee of General Development Investments Ltd was considering an investment in Manaus Woodpulp Corporation in June 1976. The Committee had also to decide how to divide any investment made between equity participation and debt. The Brazilian Government would not allow the proportion of equity to rise above half of the contribution of any single investor.

General Development Investments Ltd was formed in 1973 to channel the overseas investment activities of a number of British Unit Trusts. The company was under charter to concentrate on developing countries, and was to consider profitable long-term direct investment as well as portfolio investments. The policy of the investment committee had been to concentrate on a moderate number of major direct investments, geographically diversified, and industrially diversified. The range of amounts invested in such direct investments had been from two to fifteen million pounds or the equivalent.

The Manaus Woodpulp Corporation had commenced construction in 1975, and the construction work was on time schedule in mid-1976. The MWC was formed to exploit the major resources of Northern Brazil, and to do so in a fashion that would generate foreign exchange by exporting the woodpulp and cellulose products.

The investment programme had exceeded preliminary cost estimates as of mid-1976 but the managers of MWC believed economies in the residue of the construction phase might recoup this preliminary excess. The basic financial projections for the venture are shown in Exhibit 1. The figures in the 1975 column were actual amounts (in $US thousands) but all the rest were projections. It is notable that a positive net present value is shown, for both the equity investment and the total investment, at a 10 per cent discount rate.

There were a number of uncertainties in the figures in Exhibit 1, however. The chief analyst felt that the main uncertainties were those listed below.

UNCERTAINTIES IN THE ANALYSIS

1. The aggregate investment in cruzeiros was uncertain because it was divided among currencies which might revalue or devalue before the costs were incurred. The investment would be divided as follows, among currencies. The percentages were computed using the exchange rates prevailing in 1974.

Brazilian cruzeiros	85%
Swedish kroner	7
U.S. $	4
Deutschmarks	3
U.K. £	1
	100%

The total investment would lie between U.S. $350m and U.S. $420m.

2. The manufacturing cost estimates in Exhibit 1 were not very definite. Some labour

contracts had yet to be negotiated, and the basic material, timber, was the subject of an active and fluctuating commodity market.

3. The aggregate investment might be subject to further changes (additional to 1 above) of up to 11 per cent because the suppliers of the machinery were unwilling to quote very far ahead. If the price went up, in the suppliers' own currency, however, they would supply credit of equal amount at the normal rate of 11 per cent.

4. The 'mill harbour price' for the main product was not known. It was expected to lie in the range U.S. $250 to U.S. $305 per ton, for export. The home sales price was known to be $240 at 1975 exchange rates, and was fixed in cruzeiros, and home sales would be restricted to a maximum of 25 per cent of total volume.

5. The pattern of volume build-up over time was uncertain. The volume estimates in Exhibit 1 assumed that capacity of 400,000 tons would be reached in 1981. Capacity attainment in 1980 was thought faintly possible, capacity attainment in either 1982 or 1983 were believed to be quite likely though only half as likely 1981, while capacity in 1984 was believed a remote but not impossible contingency.

6. The loans to finance the project had been negotiated at 11 per cent. The principal would be repaid according to the amortization schedules in Exhibit 2. The only uncertainty here was implicit in Item 1 above, namely, the total investment needed. The ultimate holders of the debt had not yet been selected finally, but an underwriter for the whole had been appointed.

As a further example of the first uncertainty, the analyst pointed to the table of original estimates of the total investment amount.

Total	1975	1976	1977
350	88	175	87
380	110	190	80
420	110	210	100

The table showed that if the total investment overall could be expected to reach $380 millions, then $110 millions were expected to be spent in 1975, $190 millions in 1976 and $80 millions in 1977. The amount actually spent in 1975 was $135.4 millions.

THE SIMULATION STUDY

In the light of the uncertainties mentioned above, the chief analyst had instructed the head of computation to assist with the development of a simulation model for the project.

After considerable effort the results of this analysis were obtained and presented to the chief analyst in the form of Exhibits 3 and 4. The variation in the internal rates of return were quite considerable, reflecting the breadth of the variations in some of the assumptions.

For instance, in Exhibit 3, the bottom right-hand assumption tested showed an internal rate of return of 7.24 per cent. This would result if the investment total overran to $420 millions, a 20 per cent increase in manufacturing cost happened and capacity production was not attained until 1982. The rates of return presented refer to the entire project, not just the equity portion.

Each of the elements in the table was derived from a different combination of assumptions.

QUESTIONS FOR DISCUSSION

1. What should the analyst do with the numbers obtained from the simulation analysis?

2. What recommendation should he make to the investment committee, as to total participation and proportion of equity within that total?
3. If you were told that the Brazilian cruzeiro had just devalued by 25 per cent against the U.S. dollar, would you like the project more or less than before? Selling expenses, debt interest, debt retirement, and export revenues are in $U.S, all other items are in cruzeiros.

EXHIBIT 1

Most Recent Cash Flow Forecasts

	1975	1976	1977	1978	1979	1980	1981	1982	1983	1984	1985	1986	1987	1988 and following
Sales (thousands tons)				275	300	350	400	400	400	400	400	400	400	400
Price per ton export				300										
Price per ton home				240										
Home/export ratio				80/20										
Sales ($'000)				79200	86400	100800	115200	115200	115200	115200	115200	115200	115200	115200
Fixed Manufacturing				11800	11800	11800	11800	11800	11800	11800	11800	11800	11800	11800
Variable Manufacturing ($46/ton)				12650	13800	16100	18400	18400	18400	18400	18400	18400	18400	18400
General Expense				2637	2637	2637	2637	2637	2637	2637	2637	2637	2637	2637
Selling Expense (5.3% of sales)				4198	4579	5342	6106	6106	6106	6106	6106	6106	6106	6106
Operating Cash Flow				47915	53584	64921	76257	76257	76257	76257	76257	76257	76257	76257
Interest (11%)				23212	22783	20858	17943	14863	11783	8714	5634	2873	420	—
				24703	30801	44063	58314	61394	64474	67543	76623	73384	75837	—
Equity Invested	98386	49000	24000											
Debt Invested	36984	132335	41700											
Debt Retired				3900	17500	26500	28000	28000	27900	28000	25100	22300	3819	—
Equity Cash Flow Return				20803	13301	17663	30314	33394	36574	39543	45523	51084	72018	76257

1. Interest has been charged at 11% on the balance of debt outstanding at the start of each year, which is then reduced by the amortization from Exhibit 1.
2. All years after 1988 are assumed to have the same outcome as that year, but have not been considered in the present value calculations below.
3. The net present values at 10% were, for the entire project $11.0 million and for the equity investment $21.5 million, counting 1975–88.
4. The internal rate of return for the equity investment is 11.75% approximately. That for the entire project is 10½% approximately.
5. All the figures in Exhibit 1 are in thousands of US dollars, unless clearly stated as unit prices or volumes.

EXHIBIT 2

Amortization Schedules

The Cash Flow Calculations are based on following amortization schedules

	1978 II	1979 I	1979 II	1980 I	1980 II	1981 I	1981 II	1982 I	1982 II	1983 I	1983 II	1984 I	1984 II	1985 I	1985 II	1986 I	1986 II	1987 I	1987 II	1988 I
Investment $350 million																				
loan	230.0	226.1	222.1	209.2	196.0	182.8	169.3	155.9	142.5	129.0	115.6	102.2	88.8	75.3	61.9	51.3	40.7	30.1	19.5	3.8
amortization	3.9	4.0	12.9	13.2	13.2	13.5	13.4	13.4	13.5	13.4	13.4	13.4	13.5	13.4	10.6	10.6	10.6	10.6	10.6	9.5
Investment $380 million																				
loan	240.0	236.1	232.1	218.6	204.9	191.1	177.1	163.1	149.2	135.1	121.2	107.2	93.3	72.9	65.3	54.1	43.0	31.8	20.7	9.5
amortization	3.9	4.0	13.5	12.7	13.8	14.0	14.0	13.9	14.1	13.9	14.0	13.9	14.1	13.9	11.2	11.1	11.2	11.1	11.2	9.5
Investment $420 million																				
loan	270.0	266.1	262.1	246.9	231.4	216.0	200.2	184.5	169.9	153.1	137.4	121.6	106.1	90.3	74.7	61.0	48.9	36.0	23.1	10.3
amortization	3.9	4.0	15.2	15.5	15.4	15.8	15.7	15.6	15.8	15.7	15.6	15.7	15.8	15.6	12.9	12.9	12.9	12.9	12.9	10.2

EXHIBIT 3

A comparison of present values and IRR's under alternative investment, manufacturing cost estimates and volume assumptions

Assumptions (a) Export and home sales ratio 80:20
(b) Price Export: $250, Home $240

| | Investment $350m | | | Investment $380m | | | Investment $420m | | |
| | present value at | | | present value at | | | present value at | | |
	13%	18%	IRR	13%	18%	IRR	13%	18%	IRR
0% increase in mfg. cost									
1. capacity attained in 1980 (A)	−20040	− 98936	12%	− 51551	−129779	10.8 %	− 86965	−162630	9.58%
2. capacity attained in 1982 (B)	−49880	−123144	10.8%	− 80280	−153282	9.7 %	−115694	−186132	8.56%
10% increase in mfg. cost									
1. capacity (A)	−37021	−110723	11.3%	− 67422	−140861	10.14%	−102836	−173711	8.9 %
2. capacity (B)	−65111	−133695	10.1%	− 95512	−163833	9.05%	−130926	−196683	7.9 %
20% increase in mfg. cost									
1. capacity (A)	−53245	−122114	10.5%	− 88448	−156120	9.21%	−119059	−185102	8.2 %
2. capacity (B)	−80342	−144246	9.4%	−110734	176384	8.36%	−146157	−207234	7.24%

EXHIBIT 4

A comparison of present values and IRR's under alternative investment, price and export and home sales assumptions

Assumptions:
Manufacturing costs increase 10%
Capacity volume in 1892

	Investment $380m			Investment $420m		
	present value at			present value at		
	13%	18%	IRR	13%	18%	IRR
export price $250/ton						
home price $240/ton						
Exp. and Home						
Sales ratio 80:20	−95512	−163833	9.05%	−115694	−186132	8.56%
Sales ratio 75:25	−96468	−164487	9.00%	−131882	−197337	7.87%
export price $275						
home price $240						
Sales ratio 80:20	−57222	−137648	10.71%	−9636	−170499	9.52%
Sales ratio 75:25	−60497	−139884	10.58%	−95942	−172752	9.38%
export price $305						
home price $240						
Sales ratio 80:20	−7432	−103264	12.71%	−42846	−136114	11.44%
Sales ratio 75:25	−16272	−109699	12.37%	−62911	−143332	11.07%

14 Merrydale Ltd

THE COMPANY BACKGROUND

Merrydale Ltd is a recent acquisition of the large conglomerate Falco Ltd and has been placed for present organisational purposes in the Merchandising Division. Falco Ltd has extremely wide interests, ranging from finance and insurance, through building and into distribution. Its stated policy is to attract companies into the Group and to allow them to continue operations with a minimum of central control. To date, very few acquisitions have been made in the engineering field division, which is mainly concerned with distribution rather than with manufacturing.

Merrydale Ltd is a supplier of components to the electronic industry, and ten years ago was a private family business in an old factory one and a half miles from the city centre of Birmingham. Three years ago the company moved to a trading estate in the Black Country, from which point profits moved into the red. In the year of the move Merrydale broke even; the first year within the conglomerate involved a loss of £11,000 and in the last year, just reported, the loss was almost £30,000. This was on a sales turnover of a little over £300,000 and with a labour force totalling 155. Merrydale is a very small cog in the Falco wheel, so much so that the loss of £11,000 brought almost no comment from either the group or divisional headquarters. This is not altogether surprising when the capital of £240,000 employed by Merrydale is compared with the total conglomerate figure of over £20 million, and the fact that the Falco group made an after-tax profit of over £4 million.

MEETING WITH THE DIVISIONAL MANAGING DIRECTOR

The reaction to the most recent loss has been quite different. The three executives, the General Manager, Works Manager and Sales Manager, were summoned to the Merchandising Divisional Headquarters in Manchester, and there is little doubt that they feared the worst. In fact, the meeting was a pleasant one, though the Divisional Managing Director, Samuel Lines, made it quite clear that the position must be improved. In his opinion twelve months was a reasonable period in which to get Merrydale back into a break-even position, and one of the prime jobs was to carry out a comprehensive exercise into the profitability of the various products. Lines suggested that unprofitable products should be dropped and that marketing attention should be concentrated on the profitable items. The Divisional Managing Director had now decided to attend a meeting of executives at Merrydale in two months' time, at which he expected to see a statement of product profitability, some firm recommendations on the future of the product range, including the treatment of new products.

PRODUCTION AND ACCOUNTING METHODS

The executives took stock of the existing situation at the earliest opportunity. The Works Manager was confident of a reasonable level of efficiency in the factory which he had tended very carefully in the last five years. All agreed that production planning and control was effective and the Work Study Engineer, appointed four years ago, had done a first-class job in both method study and work measurement. Standard times were available for almost every production operation on every product, and the piecework method of remuneration applied to over 90 per cent of direct employees.

Reprinted from *Management Accounting*, September 1970.

The executives agreed that no dramatic improvement in operating efficiency was likely to be achieved. On the other hand, there had been doubt for some time about the relative profitability of the products. Ninety-five per cent of the sales stemmed from 150 standard products, and recent costings suggested that many of these products were sold at inadequate prices, mainly because of fierceness of competition, and because of the willingness of the larger manufacturers to subsidise part of their output.

The accountant, Frank Berry, was called in to summarise the existing accounting methods. As a relative newcomer to the firm, having joined a year ago, Berry was struggling to make an impression. The executives had deliberately recruited a middle-aged, unqualified man and regarded him as a 'reliable plodder'. Nevertheless, the accountant had made a number of suggestions, some of which had been implemented. He had recently calculated Departmental Overhead Rates for the first time and had produced a report on standard costing which was still under consideration. As part of the report on standard costing, Berry had produced a sample standard cost for one of the main-line products and had plans in hand to expand these calculations through the product range, as soon as the executives gave their approval. Within three days he supplied the following statement of the actual costs for the first 25 products for which information was readily at hand from current production records.

Product No.	Average Selling Price	Total Product Cost	Profit	Loss
02	15.2	9.2	6.0	
15	50.8	61.3		10.4
17	50.8	61.3		10.4
27	70.8	75.4		4.6
32	117.6	145.4		27.8
35	224.2	238.8		14.6
36	282.1	288.8		6.7
40	272.9	234.2	38.8	
41	368.3	393.3		25.0
42	355.0	347.1	7.9	
51	51.7	52.1		0.4
67	16.7	13.8	2.9	
73	208.8	209.6		0.8
74	228.8	233.8		5.0
76	6.7	7.3		0.6
82	215.8	220.4		4.6
92	195.0	224.2		29.2
93	242.5	258.8		16.3
95	81.7	95.0		13.3
100	7.9	5.8	2.1	
107	7.9	6.7	1.2	
137	132.5	117.5	15.0	
402	275.0	285.0		10.0
403	275.0	268.3	6.7	
404	275.0	268.3	6.7	

(all figures in pence)

The statement was examined and there was a general air of disbelief. The General Manager noted that, if the instructions of the Divisional Managing Director were followed, 16 lines from the first 25 products should be dropped. The Works Manager, Frank Key, was so alarmed at the figures that he insisted on a detailed explanation of the costing procedures which had been used. Berry outlines the procedure as follows:

1. 'For material costs, I work from the product specification, adding what I think are reasonable allowances for waste, then I extend these quantities at the current prices.'
2. 'For labour costs, I check on the most recent batch made, satisfy myself that all the

operations on the product specification have been carried out, and take the labour cost per unit from the batch order.'

3. 'For overheads, I use the Departmental Overhead Rates which I showed you recently and which are revised annually. Administration, selling and distribution costs are recovered as a percentage of works cost.'

4. Frank Key made a special point of asking Berry about production rejects and Berry explained that he kept some figures summarising inspection records and that he included the current reject rate in the unit product cost.

Berry made it clear to the three executives that Merrydale did not have a system of product costing which threw out the figures regularly, but that any request which they made for product costs called for an *ad hoc* exercise which he carried out along the lines indicated. As far as he was concerned the product cost statement was reasonably accurate, but he felt that his ideas on standard costing should be implemented without delay.

The three executives were undecided.

1. Should they rely upon the statement as presented and work out the marketing policy based on these figures?
   or
2. Should they wait until Berry had implemented his ideas on standard costing?

At this point the reader is invited to consider what action he would recommend.

The Sales Manager had serious doubts about his ability to assess product profitability from the figures supplied, and suggested that they should seek some outside help in order to obtain a proper interpretation of the situation. It was at this point that the three executives agreed to take the opinions of James Martin, a management consultant and friend of Frank Key.

Martin was familiar with the firm and its procedures. He was supplied with a file of working papers by Berry which included:

The total product cost statement;

a sample standard cost for one main-line product.

THE APPROACH OF THE CONSULTANT

Martin studied these details and quickly concluded that the total product cost statement might be misleading as it stood. Indeed, he thought that even if a total *standard* product cost statement was produced it would still not represent reliable and relevant information for assessing product profitability. He would be surprised if all 25 products were not making some contribution towards overhead expenses, in which case to drop any of the products might well worsen the company situation.

The first sample standard cost for one main line product included overhead standard costs arising in the six manufacturing departments through which the product passed. This overhead standard cost represented the absorption of total overhead into the cost of the product, and was based upon the budgeted total overhead costs for a budgeted level of activity. Martin felt that the latter was a snag, that he needed to use a cost per unit which would not vary with the level of activity and to achieve this it was necessary to calculate a variable or marginal standard overhead cost.

He went back to the Department Cost Analysis which had been used to calculate departmental overhead rates, and studied the behaviour of each cost item in turn.

Some items he quickly classified as fixed or period costs such as supervision, rent and rates, depreciation of fixed assets. Other items required much closer examination, and he found it useful for these items to show graphically the relationship between cost and activity.

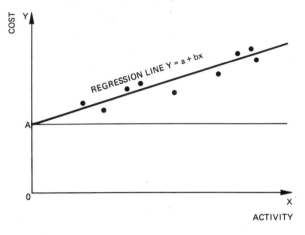

Relationship between Cost and Activity

REGRESSION LINE Y = a + bx

COST

Y

A

0

X

ACTIVITY

a (The Regression Constant) represents Fixed Costs

b (The Regression Coefficient) represents Marginal or
Variable Costs

Using the least squares method he was able to distinguish between the fixed and variable element of each item of cost. He was now in a position to concentrate on the standard marginal costs of products, which would be constant irrespective of varying levels of activity. In respect of the same 25 products, he insisted on decisions being taken regarding standard material cost and standard labour cost. The large amount of work measurement which had already been undertaken at Merrydale helped the calculations of standard labour costs, and made it possible to calculate departmental variable overhead rates on a time basis. Standards were established for production rejects and after three weeks a new product cost statement emerged.

EXPLANATION OF THE REVISED STATEMENT

Martin introduced the statement by making the point that, in his opinion, in this situation, the most relevant way to look at product profitability was on a standard contribution basis. His first argument was that no product made a profit but that each product made some sort of contribution towards fixed overheads and profit. It was important to establish the amount of the contribution, preferably on a standard cost rather than an actual cost basis, since factory inefficiencies should not, he suggested, be allowed to confuse the issue. It was tempting when product contributions had been calculated to relate those contributions to product selling prices to obtain a ratio or measure of profitability, but this was not accurate. He argued that contribution should be related to the resource which was the limiting factor in the business at that time. This might be material, such as was currently the case with nickel which should be contracted. In future, he suggested particular class of labour which was difficult to obtain, but it might be space or capital. His summing up of the Merrydale situation was that they were busy fools, since capacity and facilities were almost fully used in every department and yet they were making losses. In his opinion, the standard contribution of each product should be related to the standard production time, and this he had done on the statement. Then he had ranked the products according to the standard contribution per hour which they made. The results had been quite

Comparison of Product Standard Marginal Costs with Selling Prices

Product Number	Average S.P.	Standard Marginal Cost	Standard Contribution	Total Standard Time	Standard Contribution per hr.	Contribution Classification
	pence	pence	pence	(hrs)	pence	
137	132.5	87.5	45.0	.366	123.0	A
74	228.8	158.5	70.3	.67	104.9	A
73	208.8	151.7	57.1	.67	85.2	A
40	272.9	174.2	98.7	1.17	84.4	A
2	15.2	6.9	8.3	.106	78.3	A
67	16.7	9.9	6.8	.1	68.0	A
100	7.9	4.2	3.7	.065	56.6	B
403	275.0	198.3	76.7	1.3	59.0	B
404	275.0	198.3	76.7	1.3	59.0	B
42	355.0	262.1	92.9	1.92	48.4	B
82	215.8	160.4	55.4	1.25	44.3	B
51	51.7	36.3	15.4	.366	42.1	B
41	368.3	293.3	75.0	1.84	40.8	B
402	275.0	216.7	58.3	1.456	40.0	B
107	7.9	5.0	2.9	.077	37.7	B
93	242.5	193.5	49.0	1.45	33.8	B
92	195.0	164.2	30.8	1.07	28.8	C
36	282.1	218.8	63.3	2.3	27.5	C
35	224.2	178.8	45.4	2.0	22.7	C
27	70.8	56.7	14.1	.706	20.0	C
76	6.7	5.4	1.3	.078	16.7	C
32	117.6	110.4	7.2	.486	14.8	C
17	50.8	46.1	4.7	.54	8.7	C
15	50.8	46.1	4.7	.54	8.7	C
95	81.7	73.7	8.0	93	8.6	C

staggering, with a top rate of contribution per hour of 123p and a bottom rate of 8.6p, the latter being almost equivalent to no contribution at all.

He suggested that the statement now gave a clear picture of those products which should be pushed and which should be contracted. In future, he suggested that Berry should connect the monthly sales analysis figures with the standard marginal product costs and the revised statement would then be a useful tool in determining the production/sales strategy of the company.

Martin was also keen to explain the three contribution classifications A, B and C on the statement. Contribution classification A, he said represented those products which made a contribution better than 60p per production hour. This contribution rate represented a return of more than 20 per cent on the capital employed by the company. Contribution classification B, he explained, bore contribution rates between 33p per hour and 60p per hour, the 33p rate being a break-even rate of return. Contribution classification C included products making contributions of less than 33p per hour, that is less than break-even rate.

The General Manager said that he found the exercise novel and easy to understand. He confessed that the fluctuations of unit cost with changing volume had always confused him. He asked Martin to explain how the 33p and 60p contribution rates per hour had been calculated. Martin said that these were not precise rates, but the 33p rate was the result of dividing the annual fixed cost bill of approximately £60,000 by the annual figure of production hours available, 180,000. The 60p rate had been arrived at by dividing the £60,000 fixed costs plus a £48,000 profit budget by the 180,000 production hours.

OTHER ADVANTAGES OF THIS APPROACH

The Sales Manager asked whether this approach could be used when considering adding new products to the range. Martin replied that, in his opinion, new products should only be introduced if they could be classified A or B in the reasonably foreseeable future. The Sales Manager thought this procedure might be unduly restricting, and argued that even Class C products made some contribution which might otherwise be missed. Martin justified his opinion by pointing out that the calculation of the marginal cost figures was not a black-and-white affair. Some arbitrary allocations and apportionments were unavoidable and it was only reasonable business conservatism to cover this point by expecting some acceptable minimum above marginal costs. The acceptable minimum would also take into account that the addition of a product might well involve some slight increase in fixed costs, such as sales promotion or product design, and that the management team would have yet another problem to consider. The Works Manager, Frank Key, thought that this approach should help him to control costs. He had noted that the standard marginal costs were those that fell within the control of Departmental Managers, and he hoped that Berry would produce statements which not only dealt with product profitability but also assisted shop floor control. It seemed to him that the same basic data could be used for a for a number of purposes. Martin agreed with these points and suggested also that the isolation of fixed costs should help senior management to appreciate their significance and to assist their control.

THE REACTION OF THE DIVISIONAL MANAGING DIRECTOR

The General Manager thanked Martin for his speedy and helpful advice. Frank Berry was asked to continue the exercise for the remaining standard products, and in the meantime they would consider the action which should be taken consequent upon the revised information. A copy of the revised statement was sent to Samuel Lines, the Divisional Managing Director.

At the meeting of executives, the General Manager explained to Lines what had taken place, and was quick to point out the benefits which had already stemmed from the product profitability exercise. He mentioned that the selling prices of certain products had been increased, with more or less certainty that this would not have any effect on the volume of sales of these products, that value analysis work was being carried out on several of the products in order to improve the contributions, and it was already clear that this would meet with some success. All of this was very interesting to Lines, but he asked if he might see Martin in order to discuss the costing work.

When Martin arrived, Lines told him that he was intrigued by the exercise, though he felt that it has been made unnecessarily complicated. He said that his own background was mainly in distribution, and he believed the basic idea to be sound since it was very similar to the gross profit approach, used in the distribution industry. For years, he said, it had been customary in his Merchandising Division to assess product profitability on the basis of the gross profit percentage of sales. He used as the examples in support of his argument product numbers 137, 41 and 95 on the standard marginal cost statement. The contribution percentages to sales came out at 34 per cent, 20 per cent and 10 per cent respectively.

Martin reacted strongly to this, saying it was sheer coincidence that the figures came out in this particular way. He suggested that Lines should also look at product numbers 137 and 40, where the contribution percentages were 34 per cent and 36 per cent respectively, yet the contribution rates per hour were very different, being 123p and 84.4p. Then, there was product number 100 where the gross profit rate was even higher at 47 per cent, though the contribution rate per hour was only 56.6p.

Samuel Lines was not too sure how to answer this, but reiterated his interest in the work which had been done. 'I have just two more doubts', he said. 'First of all, I am a little worried about the way in which you've added together the various production department times in order to arrive at a total standard time. Then, what about the facts that the capital employed by each product, and the value added by the company to the raw materials cost of each product, vary considerably? The selling and distribution efforts might also differ considerably between products. Does your method of costing take this into account?'

The reader is invited to consider whether he supports the attitude of James Martin towards the new marginal product cost statement, and to consider how he would deal with the points raised in the last paragraph.

15 Newcastle Investment Co. Ltd (A)

In the autumn of 1976, Mr Smith, treasurer of the Newcastle Investment Co. Ltd, was studying a list of proposals which had been proposed by his staff for capital investment in 1977. At the next meeting of the company's directors, to be held late in October, Mr Smith would be asked to make recommendations as to which proposals should be adopted and how they should be financed.

Newcastle Investment Company, based in Newcastle, had been a large producer of diversified industrial and commercial chemicals and allied products. Founded in 1926 to manufacture certain chemical compounds used in the oil-refining industry, the company's sales volume expanded rapidly until 1931. Despite the poor position of the industry the company showed a small profit in every year from 1931 to 1935. Interest payments were met on bank loans and on a mortgage. Cash dividends, though on a greatly reduced basis, were paid to shareholders each year.

In the late thirties the company continued to expand its product line and during the Second World War it reached a position of prominence in the industry. The resurgence of demand for chemicals in the post-war period pushed the industry's and the company's sales to record levels.

In 1970 the company was reconstructed as an investment company. The subsidiaries were turned into independent operations with the investment company holding a majority of the equity and loan capital.

In 1972 the individual companies remained leading producers of chemical compounds for the petroleum-refining industry and, in addition, had diversified their product lines through the manufacture of polyethylene and polyvinyl plastics, fertilisers, ammonia products for agricultural use, and a range of commercial and household chemicals. The investment company had recently agreed to finance Heathcotes' (a subsidiary specialising in chemicals) participation in a government-industry project leading to the improvement of fuel consumption in trucks, and was considering the advisability of agreeing to finance Newcastle Chemicals' move into certain aspects of nuclear-chemical development, a development which would also be in partnership with the government.

Sales revenue for the group year in 1976 was estimated, on the basis of the current activity, to be approximately £135,000,000; a net profit of £15,600,000 after taxes was predicted.

The investment company had adopted a system of capital budgeting which required each subsidiary to submit requests for finance for those capital construction projects desired for the coming year. The project proposals contained an estimate of the funds required and an estimate of the pre-tax annual rate of return on the initial amount of the investment. Estimates of the rate of return were made very carefully, and, in recent years, had been proved reliable. The most promising proposals for calendar 1977 which had been submitted to Mr Smith are summarised on the next page.

The investment company's expansion policies were based on a desire to satisfy only those demands which seemed to be of a permanent nature, and to avoid speculative projects, however attractive they might appear. On the basis of this policy, Mr Smith did not feel that any of the listed proposals would compromise the long-range interests of the company. The investment company had been told that sales prospects for 1977 and 1978 were very promising; sales of plastics had exceeded expectations, and export sales had continued to move ahead. The management had informed the company's shareholders, in a recent letter, that they could look forward to a continued increase in

Subsidiary	Nature of Proposal	Expected life (years)	Amount	% Return before income tax
Heathcote Ltd	Computerisation of accounting and inventory control system	6	£590,000	37
	Additional chemical storage tanks	15	£8,750,000	32
Smithsom Ltd	Purchase of railroad tank cars and loading equipment	15	£1,200,000	18
	Purchase of leased space and facilities – Aberdeen	30	£4,000,000	16
Blistol Plastics	Additions for machinery	15	£5,500,000	26
Newcastle Chemicals Ltd	Replacement of power facilities, Newcastle	25	£3,100,000	14
	Construction of new materials handling system	10	£2,300,000	20–35
	Construction of facilities for loading and transfer of explosives to barges – Newcastle	10	£4,500,000	19
	Purchase of Newcastle affiliate to handle export sales and relations	17	£2,100,000	16
Newcastle Investments Ltd	Modernization of office building – re-location of functional departments	5	£750,000	35
	Purchase of adjacent office building offered for sale	27	£2,000,000	14
			£34,790,000	

sales volume and corresponding expansion of the firm for at least the next two years.

QUESTIONS

1. Do you agree with Mr Smith's view that these proposals are desirable and should be funded? Why?
2. What other information would you request in support of these proposals.

16 Newcastle Investment Co. Ltd (B)

Mr Smith knew that the proposed projects would have to be financed largely through new funds obtained outside the company. The level of earnings remaining after dividends was insufficient to finance all of the projects, so Mr Smith assumed that no more than £8.75 million would be available through internally generated sources for the 1977 proposals.

Mr Smith knew that new financing could be accomplished in several ways. The probable terms of a new share issue had been discussed with underwriters and bankers from time to time during recent months. Reviewing the possibilities of obtaining funds from outside sources, Mr Smith contemplated the following alternatives:

1. *Debentures.* Mr Smith knew, from conversations with underwriters, that it would be possible to sell secured debentures on the present market. Such a sale could be made to the public or could be privately placed with institutional investors. Such debentures would be of 20 to 30 year maturity and would carry a sinking fund provision. The cost to the company, after usual expenses, would be approximately 11 per cent annually.

Unsecured debentures, with a shorter maturity, 15–20 years, were also possible, and would cost the company between $11\frac{1}{2}$ and $12\frac{1}{2}$ per cent annually.

2. *Unsecured Convertible Debentures.* Underwriters had told Mr Smith that it would be possible to sell an issue of unsecured convertible debentures on the present market. Such an issue would carry a sinking fund or retirement provision. The cost to the company would be, after expenses, but before consideration of tax, between $13\frac{1}{4}$ and $13\frac{3}{4}$ per cent. The current price of the company's 8 per cent Unsecured Debentures was 75.

3. *Ordinary Shares.* The company's recent growth had been financed partly through the sale of ordinary shares. An issue sold in 1966 had been very successful; and underwriters thought that a large issue at £1.50 nominal value, covering the present requirements, could be sold without difficulty at a return to the company, after all costs, of £1.55 per share. At 7 September 1976 the market price was £1.62 and the cash dividend rate was 10 per cent. Shares were listed on the London Stock Exchange and were actively traded. Since 1966 the price/earnings ratio of the ordinary shares had varied from 9.5 to 13.1; the ratio was currently 10.3.

Mr Smith decided to use an overall figure of 60 per cent in computing the future impact of taxes on earnings. He also decided to use the above costs of financing, for the various alternatives, in determining the costs of obtaining outside capital.

In considering the profitability of financing a new proposal, Mr Smith had always in the past used a weighted average cost of capital – that is, the cost of the various types of equity and debt capital weighted by the proportion of each type in the company's current capital structure. The present cost of capital computed by this method was 12.1 per cent arrived at as shown in the next page.

Mr Smith took the view that the reserve account was carried at no cost, since it was available and would not have to be raised outside the company.

Mr Smith had recently attended a short course at a local business school at which the cost of financing in relation to rates of return had been the chief topic. At this meeting an economist had advanced several interesting arguments in favour of using the 'marginal cost' of capital as the criterion for determining to what extent additional

	Pre-tax Cost	Amount in £m	Weights	Weighted Average Cost
Debentures	8%	45.0	.316	2.52
Preference shares*	$\dfrac{5\%}{.4} = 12\frac{1}{2}$	.1	–	–
Ordinary shares†	$\dfrac{9.7}{.4} = 24.2$	64.5	.454	11.00
Reserves	–	32.6	.229	–
		142.2	1.000	13.52

* 12,000 shares of £1
† 43,000,000 shares (book value £1.50)

funds should be invested in productive capacity. On this basis he understood that any project which would return, after allowances for depreciation and after consideration of taxes, more than the cost of the least expensive method of financing, again after tax considerations, was a legitimate and desirable investment.

In Mr Smith's opinion, employment of this 'marginal rate' would make nearly all the projects appear desirable, since it was possible to finance the total requirements in part with secured distributors costing only 11 per cent and in part with reinvested earnings costing nothing.

QUESTION

How much finance would you make available to the subsidiaries? How profitable would you expect this financial investment to be?

17 Prendergarth Shipping Company

Mr William Thomas, President of Prendergarth Shipping Company, was considering what action he should take regarding the reassignment of one of the company's vessels in May 1964. In view of the market for ships at that time, it had become evident that the possibility of selling the vessel was not a feasible one; the ship had to be assigned to where it would best serve the company's interests.

HISTORY OF THE VESSEL

The vessel in question, the *Prendergarth Warrior*, had been purchased in October 1963. It was the only vessel purchased during the year ended 31 December 1963. In contrast with the remaining 27 vessels of the Prendergarth fleet, which were all of about 12,500 tons burden, the Warrior was a small ship of only 4,500 tons (the burden of a freighter is the weight of freight of a standard bulk it can carry). It had been acquired to allow the Prendergarth company to compete for the tapioca trade in the port of Balik Papan in South Borneo. The *Warrior* was making the voyage from Singapore to Balik Papan and back at a rate of 50 round trips a year at the present time. The freight rates on this commodity were satisfactory, but the harbour channel was such that only small vessels like the *Warrior* could get into Balik Papan to take advantage of these revenues. The cost per dollar of revenue of operating a small vessel, fully laden, was higher than would be the case for a larger ship, were the latter able to navigate the channel.

Operating costs for the two sizes of vessel owned by Prendergarth are given in Exhibit 1. The behaviour of these and other costs is discussed in Exhibit 2.

RECENT DEVELOPMENTS

In April 1964, the port authority of Balik Papan had obtained a grant to deepen the harbour channel. The plan, which had just arrived at the Prendergarth head office, showed that ships of up to 15,000 tons would be able to use the port after the deepening operation had been completed, which was expected to be in September or October of 1964. It would therefore be possible for the larger vessels of the line to be used to serve Balik Papan. The greater carrying capacity of the larger ships should, it was thought, more than compensate for the higher total operating costs of such a vessel, since the quantities of tapioca available were substantial and the demand great. The estimated costs that would be incurred by having the larger vessel deviate from the normal route to take in Balik Papan are described in Exhibit 3. The larger vessels would have to call at Balik Papan as frequently as the *Warrior* would have called there in order to fulfill shippers' requirements. If the big ships called at Balik Papan, they would have to call twice at Singapore, once before Balik Papan and once after. This was because (1) the tapioca had to be transhipped at Singapore; (2) the large vessels were usually too full of cargo on the eastward run to get the tapioca in as well before calling at Singapore; and (3) the cargo to be moved from Singapore to Balik Papan had to be loaded.

The possibility of using both the *Warrior* and the larger vessels on this route had been considered, but had been rejected because 'it would slow down the big ships too much'.

ALTERNATIVE USE OF THE *WARRIOR*

The only feasible alternative use of the *Warrior* that Mr Thomas was considering was on the route from Dar-es-Salaam (in East Africa) to Zanzibar. Some financial aspects of this alternative are discussed in Exhibit 4. At the present, the large vessels of the line called at both of these ports, incurring port charges as detailed in Exhibit 5. The Prendergarth ships used lighters in place of docking in these ports because it was less expensive and often quicker for the amounts of cargo involved. The cargo, which consisted of dates and ground-nuts from Dar-es-Salaam, and coconuts, copra, and special timbers from Zanzibar, was usually carried to the United States; the freight rates from Zanzibar and from Dar-es-Salaam to the U.S. were virtually identical.

If the *Warrior* were to be used on this alternative route, it would shuttle the cargo from one of the two ports to the other, so that the large vessel need make in future, only one call in the area on a given run, thereby saving time and portage dues. The portage dues incurred by the *Warrior* at the two ports would have to be considered, of course. The freight normally collected at the two ports amounted to about 3850 tons per pair of calls.

THE PROBLEM

Mr Thomas was anxious to arrive at a decision between the two possible assignments of the Warrior within the next few days, rather than wait until the problem became critical in the fall. The reason for the haste was that an opportunity had arisen to move the *Warrior* from Singapore to Zanzibar with a cargo which would not only pay for the cost of moving the ship but would also pay for the lighterage expenses that would be needed at Balik Papan until the new harbour channel was ready. As this was a very unusual cargo, it was not thought likely that a similar opportunity would arise before the fall.

Mr Thomas was anxious to keep all the ships as active as possible, because the company had a very good reputation among shippers and had therefore been able to fill its ships all the time. This made it one of very few fully booked shipping lines in the business.

The most recent income statement of the company is shown in Exhibit 6. The year ended 31 December 1963 was considered a typical year in the company's history. Maps of the areas under review are presented in Exhibit 7.

EXHIBIT 1

Annual Operating Costs of Vessels

Item	Costs Typical for Size of Vessel	
	4,500 Tons	12,500 Tons
Payroll	$143,594	$210,877
Depreciation	222,956	363,228
Repairs	40,000	47,500
Overhead costs	8,225	16,900
Stores and provisions	32,657	39,283
Insurance	36,030	46,750
Miscellaneous	4,750	5,625
Total Annual Cost	$ 488,212	$ 730,163
On the average, there were 345 operating days in a year, so the cost per operating day was	$ 1,415	$ 2,116
In addition, bunkering costs (fuel costs) were incurred amounting to	$ 0.73 per mile	$ 1.27 per mile

EXHIBIT 2

Discussion of Cost Behaviour

Cost Item	Behaviour of Cost
Payroll	Payroll expense is, in the short run, a fixed item. The complement of the ship is virtually fixed over a year, and in the course of one voyage it is completely fixed. No change in union rates is expected in the near future.
Depreciation	Depreciation is charged on a straight-line basis on the original cost of the vessel.
Repairs	This amount varies randomly. The figures shown are the average annual amounts expended in the industry on ships of the sizes indicated.
Overhead	This includes all expense items incurred on board the vessel, and is fixed.
Stores and Provisions	This varies with the payroll, and is therefore virtually fixed.
Insurance	There is fixed charge of $ 30,000 per ship annually, plus an annual charge of $ 1.34 per ton.
Miscellaneous	Fixed
Bunkerage	Fuel costs will depend on the routes being travelled, as the price of fuel varies to some extent from place to place. For calculation purposes, however, the figures shown may be taken as suitable averages.

EXHIBIT 3   Prendergarth Shipping Company

Calls at Balik Papan by Large Vessels   May 1964

Since the normal terminal point of the voyages of the larger vessels was Singapore on the eastward run, and since Balik Papan was further east than Singapore, it would have been necessary for the large vessels to make a round trip in order to call at Balik Papan. The feasibility of additional calls at Brunei, Djakarta, and other ports had not been investigated, but it was thought that these were not likely to be profitable.

The distance from Singapore to Balik Papn by the best navigable route was 480 sea miles, or 960 sea miles round trip. At the normal sailing speed of the larger vessels in these waters of 16 knots, they required about 60 hours' steaming time for the round trip, or $2\frac{1}{2}$ steaming days approximately. This compares with the slightly less than $3\frac{1}{2}$ days that the *Warrior* required.

The capacity of the larger vessels was such that 6850 tons of tapioca could be carried on each voyage from Balik Papan to Singapore, as against the 3,950 tons that the Warrior could take. It was thought that the bookings of manufactured goods that were currently being taken from Singapore to Balik Papan by the *Warrior* would be the same for the larger vessels; there were no indications that any additional bookings could be obtained. The *Warrior* had been carrying 3150 tons of manufactured goods on a typical voyage from Singapore to Balik Papan, at an average rate of $2.70 per ton. The difference in tonnage between the tapioca and manufactured goods was caused by the relative bulk of the two types of cargo.

The current freight rates for tapioca, amounting to $ 5.10 per ton for the trip from Balik Papan to Singapore, seemed likely to remain in force for some considerable time. Most of the tapioca was sent out on contracts, and there appeared to be a constant or increasing demand for the commodity. While the rate might go up in the future, it was reasonable to assume that it would not go down.

The turnround time (the period between the ship's arrival at a port and departure from it) at Balik Papan was relatively slow. Because of the inadequacy of the cranage facilities, it would take three days to turn one of the large vessels as against $2\frac{1}{2}$ days to turn the *Warrior*. This difference was caused by the greater amount of cargo to be moved in the larger vessels.

Because of the extensive facilities at Singapore, all ships of the size being considered could be turned round in one day at that port, regardless of the amounts being loaded or discharged.

EXHIBIT 4

Calls at Zanzibar and Dar-es-Salaam   May 1964

The cargoes that were shipped from these ports were made up of the five commodities listed below. The rates shown were those for shipping one ton of the commodity from either port to the United States, and the tonnage listed was the average amount of each commodity that had been carried per voyage in all voyages in the last six months. The remaining capacity of the larger vessels was used by freight from other ports. The large vessels collectively called at each of the two ports 80 times a year.

Commodity	Port	Rate per ton	Average Tonnage
Dates	Dar-es-Salaam	$88	500
Ground-nuts	Dar-es-Salaam	84	850
Coconuts	Zanzibar	74	400
Copra	Zanzibar	66	1,600
Special timbers	Zanzibar	65	500

The turnround time in Zanzibar had averaged two days for the larger vessels, and the use of the *Warrior* would not shorten this. This turnaround at Dar-es-Salaam had been two days with the larger vessels; the *Warrior* could be turned in one day.

The sailing time between the two ports was very short, and this distance (72 miles) was such that only one day (two days round trip) was involved no matter which vessel was being used. The higher speed of the larger vessels had no noticeable effect over such a short trip. It was thought that an overall saving of three days per voyage would be attained by the large vessels (one port call and a day of steaming in transit) if the *Warrior* were used on the Zanzibar / Dar-es-Salaam run.

If the *Warrior* were to be used as a 'shuttle', it would be necessary for scheduling purposes to have the larger ships call at the same port each time. It would be impractical to try to arrange for the large ships to call at whichever port the *Warrior* had most recently served, because of complications in the booking of freight at other ports which would be called on subsequently.

The larger ships passed through the area with sufficient frequency to permit the *Warrior* to shuttle as frequently as it could.

EXHIBIT 5

Cost of Calling at Ports

Cost Item	Varies with	Units	Balik Papan	Singapore	Zanzibar	Dar-es-Salaam
Portage dues	Tonnage	$ / day in port / ton burden	0.14	0.20	0.13	0.31
Lighterage*	Freight moved	$ / ton of freight moved	0.25	0.16	0.14	0.15
Stevedoring	Freight moved	$ / ton of freight moved	0.56	0.32	0.32	0.32
Lighthouse	Fixed	$ / visit	73.0	126.0	–	62.0
Cranage	Freight moved	$ / ton of freight moved	†	0.14	0.13	0.13
Special assessment			‡			

* Lighterage expense is the cost of having small barges called lighters come alongside the vessel in order to facilitate loading and unloading of cargo. The Balik Papan lighterage charge is for ships anchoring in the harbour channel; having lighters come out to the channel mouth would involve a charge of $0.25. Portage dues are required on entering a port and are independent of the above charges.

† There is no cranage charge at Balik Papan because the freight is manhandled. This considerably increases the charge for stevedoring relative to other ports.

‡ All ships exceeding 8000 tons burden were to be assessed $2000 for each port call (in addition to portage channel that these ships required).

EXHIBIT 6

Prendergarth Shipping Company

Income Statement for the Year to 31 December 1963

Voyage revenues for the year	$49,661,000
Voyage expenses	33,480,000
Gross margin	$16,181,000
Shore support expenses	6,318,000
Administrative and other expenses	3,916,000
Net income before tax	$ 5,947,000
Income tax expense	3,088,000
Net income	$ 2,859,000

Exhibit 7
Maps of Areas relevant to the Assignment
of the *Prendergarth Warrior*

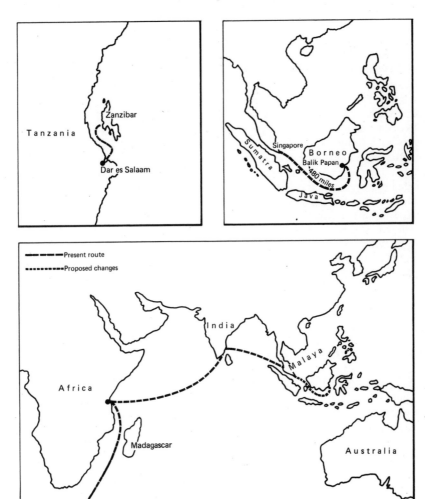

18 TAC Construction Materials Ltd

TAC Construction Materials Ltd is one of six U.K. manufacturing subsidiaries of the Turner & Newall Group. The company manufactures products for the construction and engineering industries; thermal and electrical insulation materials; bricks and pipes. It has approximately 4500 employees in eight factories which are organised in four divisions, (i) Building and Insulation, (ii) Pipes, (iii) Engineering Materials, and (iv) Bricks and Blocks. TAC manufactures over 20,000 unique products which are formed into 100 Family Groups which are further combined to produce 12 Product Sectors e.g. Roofing and Cladding products. This classification is demonstrated in Exhibit 8. The senior management organisation of the company is given in Exhibit 1.

The accounting system now in operation at TAC has been developed over a number of years but substantial changes were formulated and introduced by the Accounting Development section of the Management Accounting Department in the period 1970–3. It was introduced 'to convert a financial accounting system to a system of management accounting using standard costing and budgetary control at all levels, historical costs not being considered particularly helpful'. 'A number of benefits were expected to accrue from the system, the most important being the identification of strategies in marketing, distribution and manufacturing, the provision of a channel of communication within the firm and an aid in decision-making.'

A physical description of the system can be conveniently divided into two parts. The first part describes how standard costs and budgets are assembled and the second part shows the uses to which they are put and the reports on actual performance that they help to prepare.

PREPARATION OF STANDARD COSTS

For the purposes of this system 'product standard cost' is defined as 'a realistic assessment of product cost from the time when raw materials enter the process to the point where the product passes into warehouse stock, assuming a degree of 'stretch' in plant and labour performance'. The standards are not attainable without this 'degree of stretch' in performance. They are therefore not regarded by senior management as a strict measure of maximum efficiency but as reasonably defined objectives. Production management participate in the setting of standards and comments are actively incorporated. The work force is encouraged to achieve standards through bonus schemes and salaried staff 'would hope that meeting standards would improve the merit content of salary and ultimately secure promotion'.

The first step in the assembly of standard costs is the collection of data. The following are definitions of the terminology used and the sources of the data:

Materials

Standard quantity is the quantity of an individual item of material used in the furnish and it is obtained from the research department (Quality Control).

Standard price is the purchase cost of a unit of material and this comes from the buying department.

Standard allowance is the percentage of material allowed for scrap and spoilage. It is provided by the Works Manager in cooperation with the departmental managers and is approved by the Manufacturing Manager.

Labour

Standard manning is the number of operatives required for a job. This is also provided by the Works Manager and approved by the Manufacturing Manager.

Standard rates of pay are made available by the Manager, Industrial Relations, as per industry-wide agreements.

Standard performance is the agreed level of plant and labour performance established between the Works Manager and the Manufacturing Manager. Plant performance is derived from recent trends in historical performance with reference to expenditure on the improvement of plant efficiency. Labour performance is determined from historical performance, supplemented by the results of methods studies.

Manufacturing Overheads

Data on overheads come from production department budgets. Direct expenses fall under about 34 headings, and allocated expenses under about 14 service budget centres (see Exhibit 2). An expense is classified as fixed, variable or semi-variable as it is identified.

Authorised capacity, i.e. standard capacity, is determined by the Board of Directors with reference to initial investment decisions.

Machine hour rates (£s of overheads per machine hour) and direct labour rates (% overheads to wages) are calculated in separate categories for variable and fixed expense recovery for each department. Direct labour rates are calculated separately for individual production areas.

Processing Input Data

The data are then processed to produce product standard costs. The company manufactures over 20,000 unique products for which standard costs must be calculated. In some instances, it uses 'unit of cost' to eliminate excessive product items, e.g. a range of sizes of asbestos-cement corrugated sheets are produced and hence a cost

Process	Material Cost £	Direct Labour Cost £	Variable Overhead Cost £	Marginal Cost £	Fixed Overhead Cost £	Standard Cost £
1						
2						
Stage 1						
3						
4						
5						
Stage 2						
6						
Stage 3						
7						
8						
Stage 4						
9						
Total						

per sq. yd. of $\frac{1}{4}''$ thick corrugated sheet is calculated. An example of the determination of this product cost is given in Exhibit 3.

Advantage is also taken of the manner in which work is physically organised to use 'group cost performance', i.e. when a number of fittings are produced for a product by a group of employees, the group performance is used to determine product cost. This allows input data to be gang-punched.

All product costs are calculated annually on the TAC computer and the information is presented on one form. The full standard product cost is tabulated showing sub-totals at each production stage where the product could be at rest and form part of the production work-in-progress. These sub-totals are therefore used to calculate the value of work-in-progress. Product standard costs are subdivided in elements to show marginal costs which are used in contribution costing and, very selectively, in pricing decisions. The layout of the tabulation is as shown in the previous page:

The main use of product standard costs at TAC is in manufacturing cost control and the measurement of company performance, details of which follow later. They are also used to evaluate work-in-progress, finished goods stock, production passing into stock and cost of sales.

PREPARATION OF THE TRADING BUDGET

Sales Budget

The basic assumption by TAC is that the market is the fundamental constraint, i.e. that there is capacity to produce at standard cost everything required by Sales department. It therefore follows that the Sales Budget is the key budget. It is developed between the Business Planning, Sales, Marketing and Accounts departments in terms of quantity and price for each product or product family. Trade discounts are taken into account in pricing. Separate Sales budgets are developed for both the Home and Export markets for each division, split as appropriate into departments covering related products. These, then, form the basis of managerial accountability by department, divisional accountability and, ultimately, company accountability. They are also the fundamental basis for all other budgets and accounts.

Production Budget

The Sales Budget having been agreed, it is then adjusted to produce a Production Budget. The principal adjustments are the deletion of items wholly bought out, the addition of items if the stock of finished goods is to be increased or the reduction of items if stock is to be reduced. The total Production Budget is then phased to months, and, at factory level, to weeks, to allow for:

(a) phasing of Sales Budget (for seasonal markets, etc);
(b) works phasing (for holidays, maintenance plans etc.); and
(c) company reorganisation and development

This will result in the holding of finished goods stock at higher levels at certain times and, in turn, will call for higher usage of raw material. These figures can now be calculated for each point throughout the budget period and hence, also, the finance required for them.

Standard Gross Profit

Standard costs are now used to establish standard margins of Gross Profit. This is done in one of two ways. If the product is unique the standard cost is related to the selling price. Where a product family consists of many disparate products which are, however, homogeneous from a marketing viewpoint (e.g. pipes and flues), historical results are revised in the light of changes in standard costs to develop a new gross profit rate (%) and this is applied to the sales value of the product family.

Capacity Variance

Product standard cost is planned to recover all cost attributable to the product and, in particular, all fixed costs, if standard capacity is achieved. Sales volume, which may be subject to fluctuations, is not directly related to standard capacity. It is probable that in most years sales volume will be lower than standard capacity and some fixed overheads will therefore not be recovered even if budget sales volume is achieved. There is thus a Budget Capacity Variance which may be expressed:

$$\text{Budget Capacity Variance} = \frac{Fx(C-P)}{C}$$

where F = Fixed manufacturing overheads,
C = Standard Capacity,
P = Production Budget volume.

Because sales volume and production volume are not closely linked in the very short term it is possible to have a favourable capacity variance when sales volume variance is adverse, due to producing for stock. However, in the long term, everything made must be sold and therefore over a year capacity variance will relate closely to sales volume variance.

Non-manufacturing Overheads

All establishments are reviewed to ensure that the staff employed is not excessive but is sufficient for the achievement of company plans. These are then evaluated at current salary levels and appropriate percentages added for negotiated or cost of living increases; merit awards; and promotions, less retirements. Headings of expense other than wages/salaries are reviewed in relation to planned activity in the budget period.

i. *Carriage and Distribution*

This will have a mainly fixed element relating to Stockroom and Despatch and a mainly variable element for Carriage and Freight. If all transport is hired the expense will be wholly variable but if there is an 'own fleet', fixed costs for depreciation, etc. will be introduced.

ii. *Selling Expenses*

The main overheads under this heading may be subdivided into:

(a) Fixed – Sales force, sales offices, sales administration.
(b) Variable – Cash discount, customer claims.
(c) Arbitrary – Publicity and advertising, promotion schemes.

The variable elements will relate to turnover. Publicity is included on the basis of a 'lump sum' allocation in round figures which is inclusive of publicity administration and staff, which is covered by a sub-budget for control purposes.

iii. *Administrative Expenses*

These are largely fixed in nature and are developed by the normal techniques outlined above. Special budgets are compiled to cover situations with a development content, e.g. the introduction and extension of computer systems, operational research, business planning or other management systems and techniques.

iv. *Research and Development*

The size of the R & D budget is related to the long-term plans of the company and largely determines where it will stand in 5, 10 or 20 years' time. It is therefore of high importance and, consequently, the total size of the budget is a Board decision. The detailed budget and sub-budgets are, however, produced by normal techniques. R & D budgets normally contain a high proportion of personnel costs unless there is a high cost of purchased 'know-how' in the form of royalties, etc.

Profit and Loss items

Typical items included under this heading are:

Debit – Overheads of factory areas specifically excluded from overhead recovery rates, profit improvement (reorganisation) costs, losses on sales of assets, exchange losses, interest charged on Working Capital.

Credit – Returns from investments, profits on sales of assets, exchange profits.

Other items which TAC also credit to profit and loss account, although treated differently by other companies, are excess depreciation on assets fully written down and the difference in the value of opening stocks at old standards (as adjusted) and new standards.

Trading Budget

It is now possible to develop the Trading Budget by normal accountancy using the budget components above. It can be simply expressed by:

Sales		XXX
less: Cost of Sales		XXX
Gross Profit at Standard		XX
less: Budget Capacity Variance		X
Gross Profit after Variance		XX
less: Carriage and Distribution expenses	XX	
Selling expenses	XX	
Administrative expenses	XX	
R & D	XX	XX
Trading Profit		XX
Profit and Loss Cr. (Dr.)		X
Net profit before tax		XX

Although this calculation may be done by hand, a computer package is normally used which enables amendments and re-runs to be done at speed and enhances the value of the budgeting process in stimulating thought at all levels of management.

VARIANCE ANALYSIS AND PERFORMANCE REPORTS

The second part of the system is the comparison of actual costs with standard costs and actual results with the budgeted results planned for the same period. For the former, variance analysis is employed and for the latter, a number of reports are drawn up for different levels of management. The company states its objective as 'To measure deviations from the range of assumptions embodied in product standard costs and to establish management action programmes to correct these deviations.' Variances are classified into three groups: manufacturing, non-manufacturing and sales. All are reported in a condensed form to divisional managements who act when the index of performance falls outside the range 98–102 (where standard cost = 100).

A number of reports are prepared by the company with the amount of details such as to enable effective action to be taken by the level of management receiving the report. Ultimate responsibility for the company obviously lies with the Board of Directors and the main reports they receive are the Profit Performance Report, Return on Capital Employed Chart and Trading accounts.

The Profit Performance Report (see Exhibit 4) is a comparison for each quarter and progressively of the trading account in conventional form with the budget or 'Profit Plan'. Expenses are shown in each case as a percentage of sales. Variances are calculated and expressed as a percentage of Profit Plan.

The first task is to explain in narrative the reasons for the variance in Gross Profit. This will entail consideration of sales variances and manufacturing variances. To facilitate this analysis it is helpful to develop Gross Profit in two stages:

Sales		XXX
less: Standard Cost of Sales		XXX
Gross Profit at Standard		XX
less: Production Variances	X	
Capacity Variances	X	X
Gross Profit after Variances		XX

Gross Profit at Standard for each Product or Product Group is a fundamental control. As manufacturing variances have not been introduced at this stage, variance in the Gross Profit at Standard can only arise from Sales variances. These are therefore examined in detail by the Management Accounting Department in order to isolate the variances. Sales volume variance is the difference between actual and budget tonnages evaluated at budget price. Sales price variance is the difference between actual and budget value per ton multiplied by the actual tonnage sold. The effect of these on Gross Profit will be: for sales volume, the variance multiplied by the standard rate of gross profit; for sales price, the actual variance.

When this analysis is carried out product by product the problem of sales mix is automatically included. When a broader approach is taken (e.g. by divisions) attention is paid to the effect of sales mix within the department or division.

After the variance in Gross Profit at Standard has been analysed the next step is to investigate manufacturing variances. These are split between operational variances, and financial variances, those beyond the control of manufacturing e.g. material price variance. Operational variances are entered on a standard form (see Exhibit 5) at each factory and are reviewed in turn by supervisory management, works management for each of the factories in a division, and at Divisional level. The financial variances are analysed by divisional accountants before they are presented at Divisional Management meetings.

Non-manufacturing overheads are examined by departments in the conventional manner (see Exhibit 6). They are classified as those due to variation in turnover and those due to other causes. Other causes, in turn, are analysed between controllable and non-controllable. Examples of these three groups are (i) carriage, (ii) publicity (controllable) (iii) negotiated wage increases (non-controllable).

Return on Capital Employed is built up from a series of sub-ratios in such a manner as to show clearly the components of capital and of profit (see Exhibit 7). The capital is analysed between current and fixed assets, each appropriately sub-analysed. The rate of turnround of net total assets is then developed, leading to the master ratio of R.O.C.E. These forms are completed for the company as a whole and for each trading division.

Finally, Trading Accounts are broken down to give financial results for appropriate areas of managerial control. At TAC monthly accounts are produced for the company and each division of the company in summary form. Factory results are produced each month in the same format (see Exhibit 7). At quarterly intervals a full set of Management Accounts are produced (see Exhibits 8 and 9) which give full details of sales performance by market sector and product group. In addition, areas of distribution, selling and administration resources are reported by budget centre. Lastly, trading accounts, to net profit, are produced for all export activity, divided into divisions, together with a statement of contribution to fixed expense arising from those exports.

Comment on the extent to which the product costing system of TAC Construction Materials Ltd., is appropriate and useful for:

(*a*) measuring cost control performance;
(*b*) measuring corporate performance;
(*c*) evaluating work-in-progress and finished goods stock;
(*d*) evaluating production flows and the cost of goods sold;
(*e*) helping the marketing department to arrive at pricing decisions;
(*f*) controlling and monitoring the performance of individual managers.

In considering the usefulness of the system, pay particular attention to the assumptions inevitably made in arriving at the budget and actual, gross and net profit figures.

EXHIBIT I

MANAGEMENT STRUCTURE OF TAC CONSTRUCTION MATERIAL LTD.

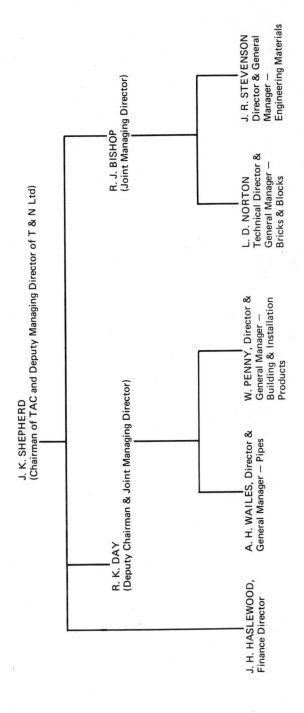

J. K. SHEPHERD
(Chairman of TAC and Deputy Managing Director of T & N Ltd)

R. K. DAY
(Deputy Chairman & Joint Managing Director)

R. J. BISHOP
(Joint Managing Director)

J. H. HASLEWOOD,
Finance Director

A. H. WAILES, Director &
General Manager — Pipes

W. PENNY, Director &
General Manager —
Building & Installation
Products

L. D. NORTON
Technical Director &
General Manager —
Bricks & Blocks

J. R. STEVENSON
Director & General
Manager —
Engineering Materials

EXHIBIT II

SUMMARY AND PHASING OF WORKS OVERHEAD EXPENSES

FACTORY

CAPACITY IN BASE YEAR

BUDGET CENTRE:

EXPENSE CODE		TOTAL BUDGET FOR 19 £	TOTAL BUDGET VAR.	FIX. £	BUDGET PHASING —MTH V £ F	—MTH V £ F	—MTH V £ F	—QTR V £ F	—MTH V £ F	MTH V £ F	MTH V £ F	QTR V £ F
21/100	Wages – Ind Reps Bldg											
21/101	" " " Plant											
21/103	" " " Int Trapt											
22	" Other											
23	Salaries											
25	Holiday Pay											
26	Mat Ins & Grad Pens											
27	Overtime Premium											
29	Pension Contribution											
30	Staff Recruitment											
32	Medical Expenses											
33	Transport of Employees											
34	Protective clothing											
36	Hire of temp staff											
39	Other Employee Costs											
39/171	" " – Sick Pay											
39/175	" " – L.S. Bonus											
39/176	" " – L.S. Function											
40/100	Ind Matl's Reps – Building											
40/101	" " – Plant											
40/103	" " – Int Trspt											
40/104	" " – Moulds, Temps											
41	" " Other											
41/125	" " – Sieves											
41/126	" " – Felts											

Code	Description
42	Hire of Plant & Mach'y
43/100	Reps & Ren'ls-O side Serv-Bldg
43/101	" " " -Plant
43/102	" " " Off. Equip
43/103	" " " Int Trspt
44	Printing & Stationery
45	Carriage-Outside Contractors
46	Rates
49/160	Purch. Utilities-Electricity
49/161	" " Gas
49/162	" " Water
49/164	" " Coal & Coke
49/165	" " Fuel Oil
50	Insurance Premiums
52	Rents Payable-Third Party
57	Licences
59	Misc Prof Services-Other
65	Publications & Tech Jnls
66	Packing Materials
68/177	Fin Goods Stock-Audit Diffs
68/178	" " W'House Breakages
72	Travelling Expenses
74	Entertaining-Others
78	Depc'n-Land & Buildings
79/140	" Plant & Mach'y Not written off
79/141	" " " Fully deprec.
82	Stock write-off-Raw materials
85	Miscellaneous
	H.Q. Expenses
	Canteen deficit
	Packages-Stock Adjustment

EXHIBIT II *(contd.)*

EXPENSE CODE		TOTAL BUDGET FOR 19__ £	VAR. £	FIX £	MTH V £ F	MTH V £ F	MTH V £ F	QTR V £ F	MTH V £ F	MTH VF	MTH V £ F	QTR V £ F
		TOTAL	TOTAL BUDGET		BUDGET PHASING							
BUDGET CENTRE	TOTAL DIRECT BUDGET											
	ALLOC FROM SERVICE B.C'S											
061	Building Service											
062	Maintenance											
063	Boiler											
064	Loco											
065	Int'l Transport											
066	Goods Inward											
067	Material Supply											
068	Handling Goods to Stock											
069	Routine Lab											
071–074	Emp., Welfare, First Aid Rooms											
075	Gen Factory Expenses											
076	Waste Disposal											
078	Mould Making											
093–098	Works Office											
	TOTAL ALLOCATED BUDGET											
	TOTAL BUDGET											

TP. & 1
OCT 73

138

EXHIBIT III

TAC. 1340
Jan. 70

PRODUCT STANDARD COST

PRODUCT CORRUGATED SHEETS
UNIT OF COST PER SQ. YD CORRUGATED
DATE OF ISSUE

SYMBOL NUMBER ....
SIZE/THICKNESS ¼" THICK
FACTORY

Latrin Ref Sheet

ELEMENTS OF COST	STANDARD PRODUCT PRICE £	PER	No OF UNITS CONTAINED IN STANDARD COST	STANDARD COST £	£
DIRECT MATERIAL Sub-accounts 101 102 103 — A.C. FINISH	0.13029	SQ. YD. FLAT ¼" THICK	1.2280		0.15998
COST CENTRE					
DIRECT LABOUR Sub-account 201					
FIBRE TREATMENT	0.00084	SQ. YD FLAT ¼" Thick	1.2280	0.00104	
PULVERISER	0.00026	"	1.2280	0.00032	
SHEETING MACHINE (CORRUGATED etc.)	0.00985	"	1.2280	0.01210	
					0.01346
OVERHEADS VARIABLE MARGINAL COST	1.93	£ cF D/LABS	0.01346	0.02598	
FIXED	2.67	£ cF D/LABS	0.01346 MARGINAL COST 0.01346	0.19942 0.03594	
PRODUCT STANDARD COST SQ. YD CORRUGATED					0.23536

1 & 2

324
526
728

EXHIBIT III (contd.)

STANDARD PRODUCT MATERIAL PRICE

DATE

ISSUE 2 1

REASON FOR ISSUE Revised of Standard Prices E.C.

FACTORY

DIVISION A.C.

PRODUCT

COST CENTRE

	RAW MATERIAL SYMBOL No.	DESCRIPTION	QUANTITY	STD MATERIAL PRICE £	TOTAL VALUE £
Standard Furnish Based on Furnish No.	TP 3269	Fibre 1	28.57	0.05238	1.4965c
	1458	" 2	28.57	0.05438	1.55364
	3592	" 3	23.8,	0.04375	1.04169
	2700	" 4	19.05	0.06200	1.1811o
	210006	Cement	800.00	0.00243	1.94400
		Hard Ground Waste	33.00		
		TOTALS	933.3		7.21693

Standard Furnish Mat. Price £0.00713 £ per -B

Standard Raw Mat. Allowance × 16.7 ℔ per SQ 40 FLAT ¼" THICK

Standard Product Mat. Price = £0.12909 £ per DITTO

Issue No 12

A.C. DIVISION

FURNISH COST PER SQ 40 FLAT ADJUSTED FOR STANDARD ALLOWANCES

%   £

MATERIAL

	%	£
FURNISH COST PER SQ 40		0.12909
SLUDGE	0.52	0.00067
BREAKAGE AND DEFECT	0.40	0.00052
TOTAL -	0.92	0.13028

EXHIBIT III *(contd.)*

TAC 1223/1
Oct. 61

STANDARD PRODUCT LABOUR PRICE

DATE ______ FACTORY ______ PRODUCT FIBRE

ISSUE 21 DIVISION AC

REASON FOR ISSUE REVISION OF WAGES RATES ETC COST CENTRE 3

OPERATION	No OF OPERATIVES	BASIC RATE PER HOUR	SHIFT ALLOWANCE	BONUS RATE PER HOUR	TOTAL COST PER MACHINE HOUR
TREATMENT	½	6/5¾d	12½% of		
			BASIC RATE		
	½		9½d	2/3¾d	
SPELLING ALLOWANCE		6/8d	8½d		
OT LS	1	6/7d	1/6d	2/3¾d	10/4¾d

STANDARDS

RATE OF MAN HOURS 1 PER OPERATING HOUR

RATE OF PRODUCTION 960 LB PER " HOUR

HOURLY LABOUR PRICE 10·3958/- × 1.05 = 10·9156/ PER " HOUR

PRODUCT LABOUR PRICE 0·0114/- PER LB

PRODUCT LABOUR PRICE £0 00057 PER LB

BASIS OF COST

LABOUR EFF. 125

OPERATIONAL EFF. 96

ROWAN BONUS ______

PRODUCTION EFF. ______

P.T.O.

A.C. Division 31 FIBRE TREATMENT PRODUCT CSR

STANDARD	FURNISH	LB	FIXED	FACTOR	FACTORISED	QUANTITY
TP 3269		23.67		0.73		26.80
1458		28.57		0.74		26.50
2700		19.05		0.73		13.91
3592		23.81		0.94		22.38
		100.00				84.01
CEMENT		800.00				
H.G.W.		33.30				
		933.3				

STD. PROD. LABOUR PRICE PER FACTORISED LB of FIBRE £0.00057

" " " " " LB of FURNISH $\dfrac{£0.00057 \times 84.01}{933.3}$ = 0.000005

PRODUCT FURNISH CONTENT 16.7 LB per 100 sq. 40 × ½" thick

STANDARD PRODUCT LABOUR PRICE per sq. yd. £0.000005 × 16.7 = £0.000084

EXHIBIT III *(contd.)*

STANDARD PRODUCT LABOUR PRICE

DATE __22__   FACTORY _____   PRODUCT __GROUND HARD WASTE__

ISSUE ____   DIVISION __A C.__

REASON FOR ISSUE __Revision of Standard Prices Etc.__   COST CENTRE __4__

OPERATION	No OF OPERATIVES	BASIC RATE PER HOUR	SHIFT ALLOWANCE	BONUS RATE PER HOUR	TOTAL COST PER MACHINE HOUR
GRADE					
CRUSHING 1	1	6/5¾d			
				2/4¾d	
OT LS	1	6/5¾d		2/4¾d	8/10½d

STANDARDS

RATE OF MAN HOURS ____1____ PER __OPERATING__ HOUR

RATE OF PRODUCTION ____1089 LBS____ PER __MAN__ HOUR

HOURLY LABOUR PRICE __8.8750/- × 1.05 = 93188/-__ PER __..__ HOUR

PRODUCT LABOUR PRICE __0.0086/-__ PER __LB__

PRODUCT LABOUR PRICE __£ 0.0043__ PER __LB__

BASIS OF COST

LABOUR EFF. ____100____

OPERATIONAL EFF ____99____

ROWAN BONUS _____

PRODUCTION EFF. _____

TAC 13221
61

144

CANDIRU FEED WASTE

STANDARD PEANUT LAGOS PRICE   £ 0.00043/-

STANDARD PEANUT PRODUCT LAGOS PRICE ﹖﹖ ﹖ TO
685   LBS
£0.0004/- × 33.30 × 16.7 ÷ 933.30 £0.00026

£55.90

EXHIBIT III *(contd.)*

TAC 1303/1
Oct. 61

STANDARD PRODUCT LABOUR PRICE

DATE ______ FACTORY ______ PRODUCT CSB. 901

ISSUE 12 DIVISION ______

REASON FOR ISSUE REVISION OF WAGES RATES ETC. COST CENTRE 9/1

OPERATION	No OF OPERATIVES	BASIC RATE PER HOUR	SHIFT ALLOWANCE	BONUS RATE PER HOUR	TOTAL COST PER MACHINE HOUR
BEATERMAN	1	6/8 d	•	2/6 d	
MACHINE DRIVER	1	6/10½ d	12½%		
R.H. CUTTER OFF	1	6/5¾ d			
TRUCK DRIVER	½	6/8 d	(BASIC RATE	HOUR – 2d	
FORK LIFT DRIVER	½	6/8 d		PER HOUR FOR	
WET WASTEMAN	1	6/3d		M/C DRIVER)	
STACKERS	2	6/5¾d			
RELIEFMAN + STRIPPERS	½	6/3d			
OT LS	7½	49/0¼d	5/11¼d	17/8d	72/7½d

RATE OF MAN HOURS __7½__ PER __OPERATING__ HOUR | LABOUR EFF _____

RATE OF PRODUCTION __3.63 TONS__ PER __"__ HOUR | OPERATIONAL EFF __195__

HOURLY LABOUR PRICE __72.6250/- x 1.05 = 76.2563/__ PER __"__ HOUR | ROWAN BONUS _____

PRODUCT LABOUR PRICE __21.0072/-__ PER __TON__ | PRODUCTION EFF __165__

PRODUCT LABOUR PRICE __0.1970/-__ PER __SQ 70 ½" THICK__ | 106.6107 SQ YDS PER TON

£0.00985

SYMBOL	MACHINE No	BASIC TONS AT 100% EFF.	AUTHORISED EFFICIENCY	TONS	PRODUCT FACTOR	STANDARD PRODUCTION TO STOCK PER MACHINE HOUR
		2.00	165	3.30	0.91	= 3.63 TONS
					:/	

EXHIBIT IV

FORM 24Q

TO   CONTROLLER–GROUP ACCOUNTING
TURNER & NEWALL LIMITED

c.c. GROUP ECONOMIST

FROM..................

....

SUBJECT–PROFIT PERFORMANCE REPORT

QUARTER TO ....

PART I

	Actual				Profit Plan				Variance Favourable/ (Unfavourable)			
	quarter		months to date		quarter		months to date		quarter		months to date	
	£000	%	£000	%	£000	%	£000	%	£000	%	£000	%
x Sales Revenue		100.0		100.0		100.0		100.0				
Cost of Sales												
Gross Margin												
Selling expenses												
Advert. & Sales prom. expenses												
Carriage & distribution expenses												
Admin. expenses												
R & D expenses												
Total Expenses												
Net Margin												
T & N service charge												
Other income/(expense)												
Profit before tax												

Inter-company sales	100.0	100.0	100.0	100.0	
Gross margin on inter-company sales					
Export sales	100.0	100.0	100.0	100.0	
Gross margin on export sales					
Licence and know-how income	xx	xx	xx	xx	

Average net assets employed, £000		
Return before tax on average net assets employed, %		

Average finished goods stocks to cost of sales	Days	Days	Days	Days	Days
Average work in progress to cost of sales					
Average raw materials and stores to usage					
Closing third party trade debtors to third party sales including VAT					
Closing third party trade creditors to third party purchases including VAT					

EXHIBIT IV *(contd.)*

PART II – Revised profit outlook for the current financial year

	Actual		Estimated		Estimated		Original Plan	
	months to date		months to year end		Full year		Full year	
	£000	%	£000	%	£000	%	£000	%
Sales revenue		100.0		100.0		100.0		100.0
Gross margin								
Profit before tax								

PART III — Comment on performance and on revised outlook
(to be continued on third page where appropriate)

EXHIBIT V

SUMMARY OF VARIATIONS FROM STANDARD COST

TAC 1049
DEC 73

FACTORY AND DIVISION ....

MONTH ENDED ....

FAMILY NUMBER															TOTAL	
PRODUCT CODE	£	£	£	£	£	£	£	£	£	£	£	£	£	£	This Month £	Cumulative £
MATERIAL VARIATIONS																
3 Good Material Instead of Waste																
4 Alternative Furnishes																
5 Excess Trimmings																
6 Sludge																
7 Breakages																
8 Process/Density/Thickness																
9 Excess Sanding																
10																
11 SUB TOTAL — Weekly Variances																
12 Material Usage																
13 Goods to Stock																
14																
15																
16																
17																
18 **TOTAL MATERIAL VARIATION**																
LABOUR VARIATION																
19 Rates of Pay																
20 Breakages/Rejects																
21 Efficiency																
22 Other																
23 **TOTAL LABOUR VARIATION**																
OVERHEAD VARIATION																
24 Efficiency																
25 Phasing																
26 Spend																
27 Capacity																
28 **TOTAL OVERHEAD VARIATION**																
29 **TOTAL VARIATION**																
PRODUCTION AT STANDARD COST																
30 Material																
31 Labour																
32 Overheads																
33 TOTAL																

	Grey Base £	Material £	Labour £	Overheads £	TOTAL £
34	Closing Work in Process				
35	Goods to Stock				
36	Transfers to other Divisions				
37	SUB-TOTAL				
38	Opening Work in Process				
39	Transfers from other Divisions				
40	SUB TOTAL				
41	NET PRODUCTION				

	Grey Base £	Material £	Labour £	Overheads £	TOTAL £	Cumulative £
Actual Expenditure						
Overhead Stabilisation						
TOTAL EXPENDITURE						
NET PRODUCTION						
VARIATION						
Capacity Employed						
(Overspendings)						
Underspendings						
COST INDICES						

153

EXHIBIT VI

OVERHEAD VARIANCE QUARTER ENDED

DEPARTMENT

ACCOUNT	QUARTER			CUMULATIVE			REASON
	ACTUAL £	BUDGET £	VARIANCE £	ACTUAL £	BUDGET £	VARIANCE £	

EXHIBIT VII

RETURN ON CAPITAL EMPLOYED

£000

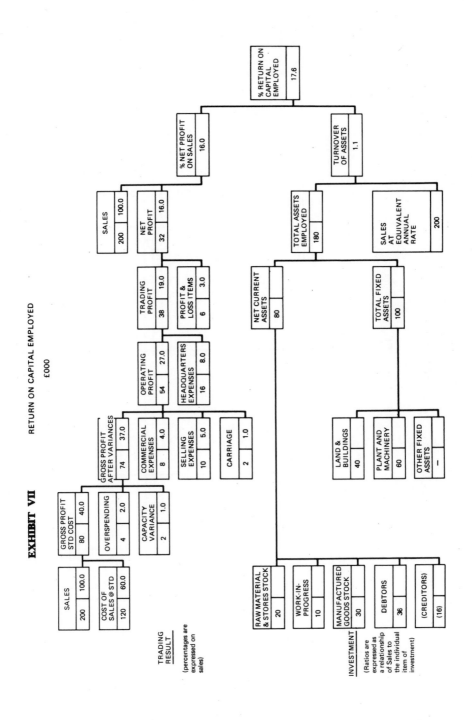

TRADING
RESULT

(percentages are
expressed on
sales)

INVESTMENT

(Ratios are
expressed as
a relationship
of Sales to
the individual
item of
investment)

EXHIBIT VIII

Building and Insulation Division

TAC Construction Materials Ltd

GROSS FAMILY TRADING ACCOUNT FOR · MONTHS ENDED

A.C.1.—SHEET No. 1

DESCRIPTION	THIS QUARTER						CUMULATIVE								
	ACTUAL			BUDGET			THIS YEAR ACTUAL			BUDGET			LAST YEAR—ACTUAL		
	TURNOVER £	GROSS PROFIT £	%	TURNOVER £	GROSS PROFIT £	%	TURNOVER £	GROSS PROFIT £	%	TURNOVER £	GROSS PROFIT £	%	TURNOVER £	GROSS PROFIT £	%
Roofing and Cladding															
Bigtix and Accessories															
Bigtix and Accessories—Thrutone															
Standard Corrugated and Accessories															
Doublesix and Accessories															
Doublesix and Accessories—Thrutone															
Doublesix M and Accessories															
Panel Sheets															
Promenade Tiles															
Slates—Thrutone															
Weatherall Slates															
Trafford Tiles and Accessories															
Weatherboard															
Cooling Tower Elements															
Other Accessories															
Sundries															
Cost Variations—Capacity															
Price															
Other															
Stock Revaluation															
SUB-TOTAL															

TAC Construction Materials Ltd

Building and Insulation Division

GROSS FAMILY TRADING ACCOUNT FOR   MONTHS ENDED

DESCRIPTION	THIS QUARTER						CUMULATIVE								
	ACTUAL			BUDGET			THIS YEAR						LAST YEAR—ACTUAL		
							ACTUAL			BUDGET					
	TURNOVER £	GROSS PROFIT £	%	TURNOVER £	GROSS PROFIT £	%	TURNOVER £	GROSS PROFIT £	%	TURNOVER £	GROSS PROFIT £	%	TURNOVER £	GROSS PROFIT £	%
Flat Sheet Products															
Flat Sheets, Semi-Compressed															
Flat Sheets, Fully Compressed															
Partition Board, Semi-Compressed															
Partition Board, Fully Compressed															
Flexible Sheets															
Asbestos Wood															
Sundries															
Cost Variations—Capacity															
Price															
Other															
Stock Revaluation															
SUB-TOTAL															

EXHIBIT VIII *(contd.)*

TAC Construction Materials Ltd

Building and Insulation Division

A.C.1.—SHEET No. 2

GROSS FAMILY TRADING ACCOUNT FOR   MONTHS ENDED

DESCRIPTION	THIS QUARTER						CUMULATIVE						LAST YEAR—ACTUAL		
	ACTUAL			BUDGET			THIS YEAR								
							ACTUAL			BUDGET					
	TURNOVER £	GROSS PROFIT £	%	TURNOVER £	GROSS PROFIT £	%	TURNOVER £	GROSS PROFIT £	%	TURNOVER £	GROSS PROFIT £	%	TURNOVER £	GROSS PROFIT £	%
Moulded Products															
Rainwater Goods, Domestic Limpet P.V.C.															
Rainwater Goods, Industrial Limpet P.V.C.															
Rainwater Goods, Industrial (A.C.)															
Flue Goods, Light Quality															
Flue Goods, Heavy Quality															
Cisterns and Lids															
Cable Conduits															
Sundries															
Cost Variations—Capacity															
Price															
Other															
Stock Revaluation															
SUB-TOTAL															
Insulation Boards															
Turnabestos															
L.D.R. Panels															
Cost Variations—Capacity															
Price															
Other															
Stock Revaluation															
SUB-TOTAL															

TAC Construction Materials Ltd

GROSS FAMILY TRADING ACCOUNT FOR   MONTHS ENDED

DESCRIPTION	THIS QUARTER						CUMULATIVE							
	ACTUAL		BUDGET			THIS YEAR				CUMULATIVE		LAST YEAR—ACTUAL		
						ACTUAL		BUDGET						
	TURNOVER £	GROSS PROFIT £ %	TURNOVER £	GROSS PROFIT £ %		TURNOVER £	GROSS PROFIT £ %	TURNOVER £	GROSS PROFIT £ %			TURNOVER £	GROSS PROFIT £ %	
METACLAD														
Aluminium Embossed Sheets and Access. 0.7mm														
Aluminium Plain Sheets and Access. 0.7mm														
Steel Sheets and Accessories 0.6mm														
Steel Sheets and Accessories 0.7mm														
Fixing Accessories of all types														
Cost Variations—Other														
SUB-TOTAL														
TOTAL BUILDING PRODUCTS														

EXHIBIT VIII (contd.)

TAC Construction Materials Ltd

Building and Insulation Division

A.C.1.—SHEET No. 3

GROSS FAMILY TRADING ACCOUNT FOR .... MONTHS ENDED

DESCRIPTION	THIS QUARTER						CUMULATIVE						LAST YEAR—ACTUAL		
	ACTUAL			BUDGET			THIS YEAR ACTUAL			BUDGET					
	TURNOVER £	GROSS PROFIT £	%	TURNOVER £	GROSS PROFIT £	%	TURNOVER £	GROSS PROFIT £	%	TURNOVER £	GROSS PROFIT £	%	TURNOVER £	GROSS PROFIT £	%
Shipsboard															
Shipsboard, Plain															
Shipsboard, Free Issue Veneer															
Shipsboard, Purchased Veneer															
Limpet Marine Board, Plain															
Limpet Marine Board, Free Issue Veneer															
Limpet Marine Board, Purchased Veneer															
Ships Doors															
Cost Variations—Capacity															
Price															
Other															
Stock Revaluation															
SUB-TOTAL															
Contracts, and Materials															
Spray Materials, Asbestos Based															
B.D. Compounds, Asbestos Based															
Spray Materials, Non-Asbestos Based															
B.D. Compounds, Non-Asbestos Based															
Spray Machine Rentals															
Cost Variations—Capacity															
Price															
Other															
Stock Revaluation															
SUB-TOTAL															
Spray Contracts															
Cavity Wall Insulation															
SUB-TOTAL															

TAC Construction Materials Ltd

A.C.1.—SHEET No. 3

GROSS FAMILY TRADING ACCOUNT FOR   MONTHS ENDED

DESCRIPTION	THIS QUARTER								CUMULATIVE								LAST YEAR—ACTUAL	
	ACTUAL			BUDGET			THIS YEAR										
							ACTUAL			BUDGET					LAST YEAR—ACTUAL	
	TURNOVER £	GROSS PROFIT £	%	TURNOVER £	GROSS PROFIT £	%	TURNOVER £	GROSS PROFIT £	%	TURNOVER £	GROSS PROFIT £	%	TURNOVER £	GROSS PROFIT £	%
TOTAL CONTRACTS, MATERIALS AND SHIPSBOARD															
Building Components															
Oxford Method Components															
Other Components															
Cost Variations—Capacity															
Price															
Other															
Stock Revaluation															
TOTAL BUILDING COMPONENTS															
Purchases for Resale															
TOTAL BUILDING AND INSULATION DIVISION TAC															

EXHIBIT VIII *(contd.)*

TAC Construction Materials Ltd

Pipes Division

GROSS FAMILY TRADING ACCOUNT FOR _____ MONTHS ENDED

DESCRIPTION	THIS QUARTER — ACTUAL			THIS QUARTER — BUDGET			THIS YEAR CUMULATIVE — ACTUAL			THIS YEAR CUMULATIVE — BUDGET			LAST YEAR—ACTUAL		
	TURNOVER £	GROSS PROFIT £	%	TURNOVER £	GROSS PROFIT £	%	TURNOVER £	GROSS PROFIT £	%	TURNOVER £	GROSS PROFIT £	%	TURNOVER £	GROSS PROFIT £	%
Pressure Pipes															
3, 4 metre and A.C. Access. up to 225mm dia.															
4 metre and A.C. Access. – 250mm to 350mm dia.															
4 metre and A.C. Access. – 400mm to 600mm dia.															
5 metre and A.C. Access. – 250mm to 350mm dia.															
5 metre and A.C. Access. – 400mm to 600mm dia.															
5 metre and A.C. Access. – 700 mm and over															
SUB-TOTAL															
Sewerage and Drainage Pipes															
4 metre and A.C. Access. – 4" to 9" dia.															
4 metre and A.C. Access. – 10" to 15" dia.															
4 metre and A.C. Access. – 18" to 24" dia.															
5 metre and A.C. Access. – 18" to 24" dia.															
5 metre and A.C. Access. – 27" to 36" dia.															
5 metre and A.C. Access. – 39" dia. and over															
Access. not related to dia. of Pipe.															
SUB-TOTAL															
Purchases for Resale															
Cost Variations—Capacity															
Price															
Other															
Stock Revaluation															
TOTAL TAC															

TAC Construction Materials Ltd

GROSS FAMILY TRADING ACCOUNT FOR _____ MONTHS ENDED _____

DESCRIPTION	THIS QUARTER						CUMULATIVE								
	ACTUAL			BUDGET			THIS YEAR						LAST YEAR—ACTUAL		
							ACTUAL			BUDGET					
	TURNOVER £	GROSS PROFIT £	%	TURNOVER £	GROSS PROFIT £	%	TURNOVER £	GROSS PROFIT £	%	TURNOVER £	GROSS PROFIT £	%	TURNOVER £	GROSS PROFIT £	%
ASBESTOS CEMENT PIPES LTD.															
Pressure Pipes															
4 metre and A.C. Access. – up to 225mm dia.															
4 metre and A.C. Access. – 250mm to 350mm dia.															
4 metre and A.C. Access. – 400mm to 600mm dia.															
SUB-TOTAL															
Sewerage and Drainage Pipes															
4 metre and A.C. Access. – 4" to 9" dia.															
4 metre and A.C. Access. – 10" to 15" dia.															
4 metre and A.C. Accesss. – 18" to 24" dia.															
Access. not related to dia. of Pipe.															
SUB-TOTAL															
Purchases for Resale															
Adjustment of Prior Periods															
TOTAL A.C.P.															
PIPES DIVISION TOTAL TAC and A.C.P.															

EXHIBIT VIII *(contd.)*

TAC Construction Materials Ltd

A.C.1—SHEET No. 6

Engineering Materials Division

GROSS FAMILY TRADING ACCOUNT FOR   MONTHS ENDED

DESCRIPTION	THIS QUARTER								CUMULATIVE								LAST YEAR—ACTUAL	
	ACTUAL			BUDGET					THIS YEAR									
							ACTUAL				BUDGET							
	TURNOVER £	GROSS PROFIT £	%	TURNOVER £	GROSS PROFIT £	%	TURNOVER £	GROSS PROFIT £	%	TURNOVER £	GROSS PROFIT £	%	TURNOVER £	GROSS PROFIT £	%	TURNOVER £	GROSS PROFIT £	%
ENGINEERING MATERIALS DIVISION																		
Electrical																		
Sindanyo Boards—Natural																		
Sindanyo Machined Parts—Natural																		
Sindanyo Boards—Ebony																		
Sindanyo Machined Parts—Ebony																		
Siluminite Papers																		
Electrofine Papers																		
Electrofine Sheets and Tubes																		
Siluminite Sheets and Tubes																		
Siluminite Machined Parts																		
Feroglas Sheets																		
Feroglas Machined Parts																		
Feroglas (Electrical) Mouldings																		
Feroform Mouldings																		
Turnalite Boards																		
Turnalite Machined Parts																		
Sundries																		
Cost Variations—Capacity																		
Price																		
Other																		
Stock Revaluation																		
TOTAL ELECTRICAL PRODUCTS																		

TAC Construction Materials Ltd

A.C.1.—SHEET No. 6

GROSS FAMILY TRADING ACCOUNT FOR   MONTHS ENDED

DESCRIPTION	THIS QUARTER						CUMULATIVE										
	ACTUAL			BUDGET			THIS YEAR						LAST YEAR—ACTUAL		
							ACTUAL			BUDGET					
	TURNOVER £	GROSS PROFIT £	%	TURNOVER £	GROSS PROFIT £	%	TURNOVER £	GROSS PROFIT £	%	TURNOVER £	GROSS PROFIT £	%	TURNOVER £	GROSS PROFIT £	%
Mechanical															
Ferobestos Sheets Non-Machined															
Ferobestos 12" Rods and Tubes Non-Machined															
Ferobestos 48" Rods and Tubes Non-Machined															
Ferobestos Silicone Products Non-Machined															
Ferobestos Transfer Mouldings Non-Machined															
Ferobestos General Mouldings Non-Machined															
Ferobestos Machined Parts															
Ferobestos Transfer Mouldings Machined															
Ferobestos General Mouldings Machined															
Ferobestos Heat Shields															
Feroglas (Mechanical) Mouldings															
Resinating															
Felt Wrapped Tubes															
Sundries															
Cost Variations—Capacity															
Price															
Other															
Stock Revaluation															
TOTAL MECHANICAL PRODUCTS															
TOTAL ELECTRICAL AND MECHANICAL PRODUCTS															

EXHIBIT VIII (contd.)

TAC Construction Materials Ltd

Engineering Materials Division

A.C.1.—SHEET No. 7

GROSS FAMILY TRADING ACCOUNT FOR .... MONTHS ENDED ....

	THIS QUARTER						CUMULATIVE								
	ACTUAL			BUDGET			THIS YEAR						LAST YEAR—ACTUAL		
							ACTUAL			BUDGET					
DESCRIPTION	TURNOVER £	GROSS PROFIT £	%	TURNOVER £	GROSS PROFIT £	%	TURNOVER £	GROSS PROFIT £	%	TURNOVER £	GROSS PROFIT £	%	TURNOVER £	GROSS PROFIT £	%
Millboard, Felt and Paper															
Felt and Paper															
Felt—Beater Addition															
Millboard—Solid Made															
Millboard—Paper Made															
Paper and Paper Tape															
Beater Addition Jointing—Solid Made															
Beater Addition Jointing—Paper Made															
Cost Variations—Capacity															
Price															
Other															
Stock Revaluation															
TOTAL MILLBOARD, FELT AND PAPER															

TAC Construction Materials Ltd

GROSS FAMILY TRADING ACCOUNT FOR   MONTHS ENDED

DESCRIPTION	THIS QUARTER						CUMULATIVE									
	ACTUAL		BUDGET			THIS YEAR						LAST YEAR—ACTUAL				
						ACTUAL		BUDGET								
	TURNOVER £	GROSS PROFIT £	%	TURNOVER £	GROSS PROFIT £	%	TURNOVER £	GROSS PROFIT £	%	TURNOVER £	GROSS PROFIT £	%	TURNOVER £	GROSS PROFIT £	%	
TOTAL ENGINEERING MATERIALS DIVISION																

EXHIBIT VIII *(contd.)*

TAC Construction Materials Ltd

Brick and Block Division

A.C.1—SHEET No. 8

GROSS FAMILY TRADING ACCOUNT FOR   MONTHS ENDED

DESCRIPTION	THIS QUARTER						CUMULATIVE						LAST YEAR—ACTUAL		
	ACTUAL			BUDGET			THIS YEAR								
							ACTUAL			BUDGET					
	TURNOVER £	GROSS PROFIT £	%	TURNOVER £	GROSS PROFIT £	%	TURNOVER £	GROSS PROFIT £	%	TURNOVER £	GROSS PROFIT £	%	TURNOVER £	GROSS PROFIT £	%
Calcium Silicate Bricks															
Facing—sand, white															
Facing—sand, coloured															
Facing—flint, white															
Facing—flint, coloured															
Facing—exposed aggregate, white															
Facing—exposed aggregate, coloured															
Common															
Sundries															
Purchases for Resale															
Cost Variations—Capacity															
Price															
Other															
Stock Revaluation															
TOTAL BRICKS															

TAC Construction Materials Ltd

GROSS FAMILY TRADING ACCOUNT FOR   MONTHS ENDED

DESCRIPTION	THIS QUARTER						CUMULATIVE							
	ACTUAL		BUDGET			THIS YEAR							LAST YEAR—ACTUAL	
						ACTUAL		BUDGET						
	TURNOVER £	GROSS PROFIT £ %	TURNOVER £	GROSS PROFIT £ %		TURNOVER £	GROSS PROFIT £ %	TURNOVER £	GROSS PROFIT £ %				TURNOVER £	GROSS PROFIT £ %
Blocks														
Standard—Normal														
Standard—High Strength														
Standard—Fair Faced														
Standard—Fair Faced High Strength														
Metric Modular—Normal														
Metric Modular—High Strength														
Metric Modular—Fair Faced														
Metric Modular—Fair Faced High Strength														
Aggregate														
Cost Variations—Capacity														
Price														
Other														
Stock Revaluation														
TOTAL BLOCKS														
TOTAL BRICK AND BLOCK DIVISION														

EXHIBIT VIII *(contd.)*

TAC Construction Materials Ltd

A.C.2—Sheet No. 1

GENERAL TRADING ACCOUNT FOR   MONTHS ENDED

No.	BUDGET CENTRE		THIS QUARTER				CUMULATIVE						Last Year Actual	
			Actual	Budget	Actual		Budget		This Year					
	NAME		£	£	£	% to Total Turnover	£	% to Total Turnover	£	% to Total Turnover			£	% to Total Turnover
	CARRIAGE AND DISTRIBUTION													
	Carriage													
	Building Products—T.A.C.													
	Contracts and Materials													
	Ships Board													
	Pipes—T.A.C.													
	Pipes—A.C.P.													
	Electrical Products													
	Mechanical Products													
	Millboard, Felt and Paper													
	Bricks													
	Blocks													
	SUB-TOTAL													

TAC Construction Materials Ltd

GENERAL TRADING ACCOUNT FOR _____ MONTHS ENDED _____

BUDGET CENTRE		THIS QUARTER		CUMULATIVE					
				This Year		Budget		Last Year Actual	
		Actual	Budget	Actual					
No.	NAME	£	£	£	% to Total Turnover	£	% to Total Turnover	£	% to Total Turnover
	Distribution								
091	Stockroom, Packing and Despatch								
099	Works Office—Forwarding								
150	Scottish Depot								
740	Traffic								
	SUB-TOTAL								
	TOTAL CARRIAGE AND DISTRIBUTION EXPENSES								

EXHIBIT VIII (contd.)

TAC Construction Materials Ltd

GENERAL TRADING ACCOUNT FOR .... **MONTHS ENDED**

A.C.2—Sheet No. 2

BUDGET CENTRE		THIS QUARTER		CUMULATIVE				Last Year Actual	
				This Year		Budget			
		Actual	Budget	Actual					
No.	NAME	£	£	£	% to Total Turnover	£	% to Total Turnover	£	% to Total Turnover
	SELLING EXPENSES								
	Building and Insulation Division								
110/115	Sales Service Departments								
116/117/121/125	Special Products								
120	Marketing								
124/128/140	National Sales Force								
122	Export Sales								
190	Commercial Expenses								
	SUB-TOTAL								
	Pipes Division								
210	Administration								
220	Regional Sales — South								
230	" — North								
290	Commercial Expenses								
	SUB-TOTAL								
	Engineering Materials Division								
310	Marketing								
320	Home Sales								
321	Export Sales								
322	Millboard Felt & Paper Sales								
390	Commercial Expenses								
	SUB-TOTAL								

TAC Construction Materials Ltd

GENERAL TRADING ACCOUNT FOR   MONTHS ENDED

BUDGET CENTRE		THIS QUARTER		CUMULATIVE					
				This Year		Budget		Last Year Actual	
		Actual	Budget	Actual					
No.	NAME	£	£	£	% to Total Turnover	£	% to Total Turnover	£	% to Total Turnover
	Brick and Block Division								
410	Bulwell Sales Office								
420	Halton Sales Office								
490	Commercial Expenses								
	SUB-TOTAL								
960-962	Publicity Services								
930	General Selling Expenses								
	TOTAL SELLING EXPENSES								

EXHIBIT VIII (contd.)

TAC Construction Materials Ltd

GENERAL TRADING ACCOUNT FOR _____ MONTHS ENDED _____

BUDGET CENTRE		THIS QUARTER				CUMULATIVE					Last Year Actual	
		Actual		Budget		Actual		This Year		Budget		
No.	NAME	£	% to Total Turnover	£		£	% to Total Turnover	£		£	% to Total Turnover	£	% to Total Turnover
	HEADQUARTERS & ADMINISTRATIVE EXPENSES											
	Finance/Administration											
710	Buying											
720	Financial Accounting											
730	Management Accounting											
750/1	Administrative Services											
810	Computer Operations											
820	Management Systems											
790	General											
	SUB-TOTAL											
	Other Headquarters Services											
910	Production Services											
911	Central Engineering											
912/13/14	Other Manufacturing Services											
915	Quality and Raw Material Control											
916	Brick and Block Project											
940	Business Planning											
970/1	Personnel											
	SUB-TOTAL											

174

TAC Construction Materials Ltd

GENERAL TRADING ACCOUNT FOR _____ MONTHS ENDED _____

BUDGET CENTRE		THIS QUARTER				CUMULATIVE						
		Actual	Budget	Actual		This Year		Budget		Last Year Actual		
No.	NAME	£	£	£	% to Total Turnover	£	% to Total Turnover	£	% to Total Turnover	£	% to Total Turnover	
	Research and Development											
610/690	Administration & Information Service and General											
650	R. & D.—Building and Insulation Products											
660	Pipes and Thermoplastics											
670	Engineering Materials											
	SUB-TOTAL											
	TOTAL HEADQUARTERS AND ADMINISTRATIVE EXPENSES											
	LESS: Amount charged to Manufacturing Cost of Sales											
	NET TOTAL—HEADQUARTERS AND ADMINISTRATIVE EXPENSES											

EXHIBIT VIII (contd.)

TAC Construction Materials Ltd

GENERAL TRADING ACCOUNT FOR   MONTHS ENDED

A.C.2—Sheet No. 4

No.	BUDGET CENTRE NAME	THIS QUARTER		CUMULATIVE					
		Actual £	Budget £	This Year				Last Year Actual	
				Actual £	% to Total Turnover	Budget £	% to Total Turnover	£	% to Total Turnover
	GROSS PROFIT								
	Non Factory Overheads—								
	Carriage and Distribution Expenses								
	Selling Expenses								
	Headquarters and Administrative Expenses								
	TOTAL								

TAC Construction Materials Ltd

GENERAL TRADING ACCOUNT FOR .... MONTHS ENDED ....

No.	BUDGET CENTRE NAME	THIS QUARTER		CUMULATIVE						
		Actual	Budget	This Year					Last Year Actual	
				Actual		Budget				
		£	£	£	% to Total Turnover	£	% to Total Turnover		£	% to Total Turnover
	TRADING PROFIT TRANSFERRED TO PROFIT AND LOSS ACCOUNT									

EXHIBIT IX

FACTORY PROFIT AND LOSS ACCOUNT

	December Qtr		March Qtr		June Qtr		September Qtr		Total	
	£'000	%	£'000	%	£'000	%	£'000	%	£'000	%
Sales		100.0		100.0		100.0		100.0		100.0
Gross Profit										
LESS: Overspendings Capacity Variance										
Gross Profit after Variances										
LESS: Carriage & Distribution Selling Expenses										
Operating Profit/Loss										
LESS: H.Q. Expenses incl. Research & Development										
Trading Profit/Loss										
ADD: Profit & (Loss) Items										
Profit/Loss before Tax										

Bibliography

A wide range of reading is available in the literature of accounting, control and financial management on topics relating to the cases in this book. Instead of attempting to list these exhaustively we have chosen to identify relevant chapters in a number of widely used textbooks.

The texts which we have chosen to include are:

Amey, L. R., and Egginton D. A., *Management Accounting: A Conceptual Approach*, London, Longman 1973.

Anderson D. R., Schmidt, L. A., and McCosh, A. M., *Practical Controllership*, 3rd edition. Homewood, Illinois, Irwin 1973.

Horngren, C. T., *Cost Accounting: A Managerial Emphasis*, 3rd edition. Englewood Cliffs, New Jersey, Prentice-Hall, 1972.

Shillinglaw, G., *Cost Accounting: Analysis and Control*, 3rd edition, Homewood, Illinois, Irwin 1972.

Sizer, J., *An Insight into Management Accounting*, London, Penguin. 1969.

Throughout the listing below, these books are identified by the authors' initials, namely: A.E., A.S.M., H, G.S., J.S., – and the numbers refer to chapters.

Associated Biscuit Manufacturers Ltd	A.E.	11, 15
	A.S.M.	13, 15
	H.	5, 14, 21
	G.S.	14, 23, 26
	J.S.	5, 6
BCM (Industrial Holdings) Ltd	A.E.	17, 18
	H.	21
	G.S.	23
	J.S.	4
Bultman Automobiles, Inc.	A.E.	17, 18
	H.	21, 22
	G.S.	23, 25
Burmah Oil Company	A.E.	4, 19, 20
	A.S.M.	19, 20
	J.S.	5
Cresta Plating Company Ltd	A.E.	17, 18
	H.	21, 22
	G.S.	23, 25
The Dalgety Group	A.E.	4, 16
	A.S.M.	17, 20
	H.	21
	G.S.	23
Elliott Products Ltd	A.E.	11, 12
	A.S.M.	15
	G.S.	26
	J.S.	6

Engineering Products Ltd	A.E.	19
	A.S.M.	13, 14
	H.	5
	G.S.	14
Fudge Creations Ltd	A.E.	11, 12
	A.S.M.	15
	H.	13, 14
	G.S.	26
	J.S.	6
Hanson Manufacturing Company	A.E.	6, 7
	A.S.M.	14
	H.	2, 3, 11
	G.S.	2, 3
	J. S.	8
James & Breasley Ltd	A.E.	14, 15, 18
	A.S.M.	13, 14, 16, 17
	H.	6, 8
	G.S.	17, 18
	J.S.	7
Manaus Woodpulp Corporation	A.E.	11, 12
	A.S.M.	15, 25
	H.	13, 14, 23
	G.S.	26
Merrydale Ltd	A.E.	7, 9, 10
	A.S.M.	14
	H.	3, 11
	G.S.	6, 9, 17, 27
	J.S.	4, 8, 10
Newcastle Investment Co. Ltd	A.E.	11, 12, 16
	A.S.M.	15
	H.	13, 14
	G.S.	26
	J.S.	6
Prendergarth Shipping Company	A.E.	6
	H	2, 3, 11
	G.S.	2, 3
	J.S.	8
TAC Construction Materials Ltd	A.E.	13, 15, 18
	A.S.M.	7, 8
	H.	6, 7, 9, 25
	G.S.	12, 15, 16, 20, 24